"What Happened at School Today?"

Also in the Good Housekeeping
Parent Guides Series

"What Happened at School Today?"

Helping Your Child Handle Everyday School Problems

Judi Craig, Ph.D.

Hearst Books
New York

Library of Congress Cataloging-in-Publication Data

Craig, Judith E., 1940–
   "What happened at school today?" : helping your child handle everyday school problems
Judi Craig.—1st ed.
     p. cm.—(Good housekeeping parent guides)
   "A Skylight Press book."
   Includes bibliographical references and index.
   ISBN 0-688-13195-6
   1. Home and school—United States. 2. Education, Elementary—Parent participation—United States. 3. Stress in children—United States. I. Title. II. Series.
LC225.3.C73   1994
370.19'312—dc20   94-4419
                                    CIP

Printed in the United States of America

First Edition

1 2 3 4 5 6 7 8 9 10

BOOK DESIGN BY PATRICE FODERO

To all parents and teachers . . .

who strive to make the school experience
for children more effective, challenging,
creative, and positive

About the Good Housekeeping Parent Guides

Children are a most wonderful gift in our lives—and they are also a challenge! That's why, nine years ago, we created *Good Housekeeping*'s largest-ever special editorial section: the Child Care section. Winner of a National Magazine Award in 1988, this annual section has grown by leaps and bounds to comprise more than one hundred pages, featuring articles from such notable collaborators as the American Academy of Pediatrics and the Bank Street College of Education.

The Good Housekeeping Parent Guides continue this spirit of helping parents meet the challenges of childrearing. Written by uniquely qualified authorities, these lively, informative books invite you to explore in-depth the everyday challenges of parenting. They are filled with ideas, examples, and strategies drawn from the real-life situations we all encounter with children. They offer new ways to understand and respond to children, as well as guidance on handling our own needs as parents.

We hope you find these guides valuable additions to your home library, providing new insights into your children, as well as innovative ideas to consider in your role as a parent. Most of all, we hope that they contribute to the loving bond you share with your child.

John Mack Carter
Editor-in-Chief
Good Housekeeping

A Note to the Reader

While I have used both male and female pronouns to refer to "the child," I've chosen to use "she" or "her" to refer to "the teacher." This is in no way meant to discount the many men who teach in elementary school, but is used for the sake of writing flow.

My heartfelt thanks to . . .

Johnny Clay Johnson, Ph.D., Clinical Psychologist in private practice (specializing in children and adolescents), for his thorough, thoughtful reading of the manuscript, for his right-on suggestions, and for being my friend and colleague whom I can always trust to tell me exactly what he thinks.

Barbara Frandsen, M.Ed., Associate Professor, St. Edwards University (teaches methodology courses for elementary school teachers and supervises their practicums and internships), and owner of Family School (a private company that provides workshops on cooperative learning, reading, and parent training), and

Sally Nelson, M.A., CCC, and Barbara Warren, M.Ed., CCC, owners of Olmos Speech, Language and Learning Clinic (specializing in diagnosis and remediation of children, adolescents, and adults who have learning/language differences), for their helpful ideas on the learning differences and special education material.

Toni Sciarra, Senior Editor, Hearst Books, and Meg Schneider and Lynn Sonberg, Skylight Press, for their continual assistance, ready availability, expert editing, and warm encouragement.

Contents

Chapter 3 · Teacher Troubles

A Parent's Bias

Common Problem Situations

Chapter 4 · When Your Child Is Having Social Problems

Common Problem Situations

Chapter 5 · When Your Child Gets into Trouble

The Behavior Contract

Common Problem Situations

Chapter 6 · When Achievement Becomes an Issue

Factors That Can Affect Your Child's
Achievement · How Do You Measure Achievement?

Common Problem Situations

Chapter 7 · Homework Hassles   141

Parents' Concerns About Homework · Establishing
a Homework Philosophy · The Study
Environment · Who's Really Responsible for
Homework? · An Effective Motivation Strategy

Common Problem Situations   148

Chapter 8 · When Your Child
Doesn't Want to Go to School   160

A Mixed Message?

Common Problem Situations   162

Chapter 9 • When Your Child Needs Special Help

Learning Styles • Learning/Language
Differences • How Do You Know If Your Child
Has a Learning/Language Difference? • Attention
Deficit Disorder • When Your Child Needs an
Evaluation • What Do You Tell a Child Who Has a
Learning/Language Difference? • What Can Be
Done to Help? • A Controversial Note • The
Special-Education Option • Professionals Who Can
Help • The Legal Option

CHAPTER 1

How to Be Your Child's Best Advocate

WHEN YOU THINK BACK TO YOUR ELEMENTARY SCHOOL DAYS, YOU might have one of two general reactions: a sense of warm nostalgia, or a feeling of relief that you'll never have to go back! More typically, you might have a mixture of positive and negative impressions.

Perhaps you loved your teachers, but had trouble with your classmates. Maybe you couldn't stand the teachers and the rules, but fondly remember that you looked forward to seeing your friends on those otherwise tedious days. Perhaps one or two teachers stand out in your memory—either as saints, or as prime examples of "everything you never wanted in a teacher." It could be that you loved learning and found your schoolwork motivating as well as challenging. Or you might have dreaded the academics, finding your studies boring, frustrating, and just no fun.

Whatever your reaction, it's likely to be a strong one. After all, school is such a central part of a child's life that it would be impossible to escape its impact. When you consider that most youngsters are in school six to seven hours a day, five days a week, you realize that school takes up roughly half of a young child's day during the school year. No wonder it leaves such a strong impression!

Now things have come full circle and you're facing the school issue with your own child. Whatever your own childhood experience, you want *your* child to have the best of all possible situations. In a nutshell, you want her to look forward to going to school, to enjoy learning, to achieve to the level of her potential, to behave appropriately, and to get along well with her teachers and with her classmates. What an expectation!

Understandably, you might approach your child's step into the world of school with a mixture of optimism and anxiety. So what can you do as a parent to help maximize your child's chances for school success?

GETTING INVOLVED

Simply telling your child that school is important is not enough. It's your actual involvement that will make her feel emotionally supported and give her the healthy message that you really care about her education. Youngsters whose parents remain indifferent to the educational process are more likely to be unconcerned about achievement, and to give up and drop out when the going gets tough. More important, a child whose parents don't "walk their talk" about being interested in their children's school experiences often grow up harboring feelings that the parent "just didn't really care about me."

Make Your Presence Felt

Certainly, this doesn't mean that you have to live at the school, bake cookies ad nauseam, be a room mother every year, or volunteer to chair every PTA committee known to man! A little of your time can go a long way.

Instead, an involvement that's healthy but not overdone can be demonstrated by doing *something* for the school, or for your child's specific class, several times each school year. Obviously, a kid loves it if Mom volunteers to be a room mother, or Dad accompanies the class on a field trip or helps out with various projects regularly. But for the majority of moms and dads who are employed during the school day, such choices may be unavailable.

Although it can take some creativity to come up with ways to demonstrate involvement if you have a greatly limited time schedule, there are still options. Some school events take place in the evening, such as school carnivals and PTA meetings. Even working parents can participate occasionally in daytime school projects by sending baked goodies for a class party or bake sale. If you are employed but have some flexibility in your schedule, you might consider going to the school occasionally to have lunch with your child. Or you might take a half-day off for a class field trip or to attend some special daytime function, such as a class play.

While you might not have time to chair a committee, you can occasionally volunteer to make phone calls, type, or lend a hand to glue, paint, or sew something for a particular project. You might also send some type of snack (with the teacher's permission) for the class on your child's birthday. Maybe you have an item on hand that would be nice to send along when your child's class is studying a particular subject; for example, an Indian artifact, a musical instrument, a small plant, an ostrich egg, and so on (again, be sure to clear this with the teacher ahead of time).

Perhaps you have a hobby or talent that you would be willing to share with your child's class. Or you might have an occupation that would be interesting for the class to hear about firsthand. Doing something like this even once in your child's school career can make a lasting impression on him that is well worth the extra effort.

Encourage Conversation About School

You will also show involvement in your child's school life by encouraging her to talk about her school experiences. Find out what she's studying, and then talk about any experiences you've had that are related. Be aware of her moods; ask if something is bothering her if she seems unusually quiet or upset (for more information, see "When Your Child Won't Talk About School" in Chapter 2). Be interested in her homework; let her know that you're available for questions and help (see Chapter 7 for more information about homework issues).

WHEN—AND WHEN NOT—TO LET YOUR CHILD HANDLE A PROBLEM

Quite often, parents decide to talk with a teacher or counselor about a problem their child is having that might be resolved by giving the *child* the responsibility for trying to work things out on her own. It's not that there aren't times when a parent needs to act, but there's such a thing as jumping in too soon.

The General Rule

Try to get your child to work things out on her own, first. Even if she's very young, you want to try to make her feel that she can go to her teacher with a problem. Exceptions would be situations where you have cause to think a teacher is being emotionally or physically abusive, or where another child at the school presents a physical or emotional danger (assault, severe ridicule) to your child. Letting your child try to work things out without your intervention has several advantages. Your child will be empowered if she is successful. She'll learn the valuable lesson that she is able to have some control over what happens in her life, and that she is effective. The benefits to her sense of self-esteem will be enormous. Also, she won't get the reputation among her peers for being a "mommy's girl" or a tattletale.

That doesn't mean, of course, that you can't do some things behind the scenes to help out your child. You can help her rehearse what she's going to say (perhaps with role playing) to the teacher or to the other child who is involved, until she's reasonably comfortable with her plan. If your child needs a little nudge to talk with her teacher, you can write the teacher a note telling her that your child wants to discuss something with her in private. Let your child know what the note says, if she's not old enough to read it herself.

You can also reassure your youngster that, should her efforts fail to get results, you will then speak with the teacher. But avoid doing the work for your child. You want to be in the position of congratulating her for learning to take care of herself.

Should You Call Another Child's Parents?

If the problem concerns another child's behavior toward your child, and your child is unsuccessful in getting results with the other youngster, it's often better to talk with the teacher (or counselor, if the other child is not in your child's class), rather than call the other child's parents (unless you know them). A call from the school letting the other parents know what's going on keeps you from getting embroiled with a parent who might feel threatened or angry. If the problem between the two children occurs out of school, then you would speak to the parents directly. However, you still might wish to let the teacher know that the two youngsters are having difficulty.

ESTABLISHING RAPPORT WITH TEACHERS

Even as a perfectly capable adult, you might experience a pang of anxiety as you prepare to meet your child's teacher. After all, you are entrusting this teacher with the care and welfare of a very prized little human being. You want the teacher to like your child, to recognize his special qualities, to help him reach his potential, and to react to him in a helpful, compassionate way. In other words, you feel protective toward your child and want him to have the very best.

Why the Anxiety?

You probably realize that a great deal rests on a good child/ teacher match. A child will often work harder and achieve more for a teacher whom he likes. Also, the teacher has tremendous impact upon a child's feelings about his capacity to learn and, thus, his self-esteem. The tenor of an entire school year is often set— positively or negatively—by a child's reaction to his teacher.

As if that isn't enough to make you feel a little anxious about meeting a teacher, you might also worry about the kind of impression *you* will make on this important person who spends so much time with your child! Thoughts like "Will the teacher think I'm not a good mother/father if my child is not doing well?" or "Will the teacher think I'm overprotective, or coming on too strong?" and "If this teacher doesn't like me for some reason, will she take it out on my child?" are common.

It's also possible that you might find yourself feeling a bit defensive, intimidated, or fearful as you prepare to meet your child's teacher, but have no idea why you feel this way. Remember, your own prior experiences in school can color your attitude toward teachers, and your unexpected reaction simply means that you've unintentionally "rubberbanded" back to your own experience.

From the Teacher's Side

As you grapple with your own fears, it's important to realize that teachers also have their own set of anxieties about parents. They are aware that many parents will blame *them* if a child doesn't do well in school. If the teacher is just beginning a teaching career, parents might perceive her as "young and inexperienced"; if she's older or has been teaching a long time, she can be accused of being "out of date and rigid." In other words, she can't win!

Also, teachers are well aware that parents can be defensive or angry at the outset because of their leftover frustration or anger toward a child's previous teacher, or because of a prior problem situation with school personnel. The tension may be further heightened because the parents are looking to *this* teacher to turn things around for their child.

Getting Off to a Good Start

Your best attitude for establishing a good relationship with your child's teacher is to assume that she has your child's best interests at heart (because she probably has). Both you and she are hoping for a smooth, productive year in which your youngster will learn well and will like coming to school.

To get off on the right foot, introduce yourself at the appropriate time, be friendly, and keep your remarks short and to the point (unless your first meeting is a conference). Remember, teachers have many students in a class, usually somewhere between twenty and thirty-two, and they appreciate a considerate parent who is sensitive to their time crunch. If you want to speak with a teacher about your particular concerns, simply ask her when it would be convenient for you to call and make an appointment. Whether you catch her before or after class, in the school hall, at an open house, or at some other school function, remember to be brief.

Even if it's not your first meeting with a teacher, be sure to remind her who you are *whenever* you speak with her, unless you are absolutely sure that she knows your name. "I'm Nancy Jones, Susie's mom" takes her off the hook from having to wrack her brain to figure out which child is yours. Remember, *you* only have to remember one name; she probably has to remember at least a couple dozen.

If you need to tell the teacher something on a particular day, think about writing her a short note. If your child is an unreliable deliverer, step into the classroom and hand it to her when you drop off your child in the morning. Make your note brief and to the point, not a tome. If you can't say what you want in a few lines, set up a designated conference time or ask the school office to give the teacher a message to call you when it's convenient for her. It's also helpful to make a habit of writing your phone number under your signature whenever you give her a note. Then she'll have your number readily available if she decides to call you later that day or evening. If your note is a *request* for her to call you, include the times you can be reached.

To Tell, or Not?

If you have a child who has any type of school problem, you might wonder whether or not to tell the teacher about the situation up front. Many parents wonder if it might be better to take a wait-and-see position. They are afraid that they might cause the teacher to expect problems with their youngster, thus encouraging the teacher to "look for problems"—and then somehow creating a self-fulfilling prophesy. Other parents never even think about talking with the teacher about potential problems, because they assume that she has read the child's school records before the first day of school.

While many teachers do read school records on all their children, many do not. If there's something in that record that the teacher needs to know (for example, suggestions from an evaluator on specific ways to help the child), it's best to call this to the teacher's attention when the year begins. Likewise, if you know that your child has a particular problem—whether academic, behavioral, or social—it's best to tell her at the start. But why?

A child who really needs special consideration or monitoring is likely to need it from the beginning of the year. If a teacher knows what to look for, she can intervene more quickly, getting the child on track sooner. If a teacher is forewarned about certain aspects of a youngster's personality and behavior (shyness, aggressiveness, tendency to argue, insecurity about reading out loud, and so on), she can sometimes use preventive strategies that might reduce the likelihood of the problem's occurence. She will also be more likely to nip a problem in the bud if she's prepared for it.

The point is, it's fairer to your child (and the teacher!) to alert the teacher in advance about any problems you think will, or might, occur. When everyone is clear from the start about what to look for and what to do about it should it occur, the child is likely to be helped sooner. Waiting until later in the year to confront the issue can result in your child's getting off to a negative start that may have been avoided.

GETTING WHAT YOU NEED FROM SCHOOL CONFERENCES

Whether it's routine conference time or a conference that has been specially requested by you or by the teacher, you'll want it to be a time for good, clear communication. It's very frustrating to leave a conference feeling confused and wondering what the teacher was *really* saying, or having questions of your own that you somehow never asked.

Getting Ready

To help things go smoothly, plan to take a notepad with you. This allows you to prepare in advance. Think about any questions you might have, and jot them down for quick reference. The pad also provides a way for you to record any notes you wish to make as you and the teacher talk.

If it's the teacher who has called for the conference, you might feel a little apprehensive. Thoughts like "What on earth could be wrong?" or "She must be going to tell me something awful if she had to call me in" or even "Oh no! Now what!" might race through your mind. Thoughts like these are especially likely to occur if you have no idea why the teacher might want to talk with you.

On the other hand, maybe your child has had a school problem in the past. If so, you probably have your own ideas about why that problem occurs. You might even think that the teacher isn't handling your child in the best way, or your child wouldn't be having the difficulty. So you might enter a conference feeling a little defensive or even angry.

No matter who has called the conference, prepare yourself to keep an open mind as you meet with the teacher. There will certainly be time for you to talk about your ideas, concerns, and suggestions, but plan to hear her out first. Remember, a conference is an opportunity for you and the teacher to communicate openly and to develop an alliance.

Communicating Clearly

As in communication with anyone, it's always best to present your thoughts and feelings in "I" messages rather than "You" messages. This means that you state what *you* think and observe rather than what you think the *teacher* is doing or thinking. For example, instead of saying something like "You give Jonathan too much homework" (or even "I *think you* give Jonathan too much homework, which is still basically a "You" message), restate your concern as "I'm worried that Jonathan has to spend so much of his time doing homework." The second statement makes your point without sounding accusatory, and is less likely to make the teacher feel defensive.

Don't hesitate to ask a teacher what she means by something she says that you don't thoroughly understand. Remember, there is no such thing as a "stupid" question. If she uses educational terms that you might not be familiar with (such as auditory sequencing, perceptual motor difficulties, visual tracking, and so on), ask her to clarify anything that you don't understand.

Quite often, the time seems to fly during a conference and you find yourself needing to end it without having talked about everything you wanted to cover or before you and the teacher have resolved anything. In this case, be aware of the teacher's schedule and suggest, "Could we finish this later by phone or set up another appointment? I feel we haven't finished." Teachers are usually glad to make extra time for the parent who is considerate of their tight schedules.

When You Disagree

If the teacher makes a remark that you don't agree with or one that surprises you, ask her to give you some examples of what she means before you jump in with your opinion. This tactic helps to make sure you and the teacher are both on the same wavelength. Then give her your ideas, using your own examples.

If a teacher asks you to do something that you don't support or are not yet sure about (for example, that you talk with the counselor about having your child considered for a special-education program), feel free to tell her that you'd like to think about what she's recommending, perhaps getting back to her the next day by phone or sending a note with your child telling her your decision. Don't leave feeling that you've been railroaded into something you're not sure about. The teacher will appreciate your honesty, rather than thinking that the two of you agreed on something and then you backed out on your part of the bargain.

Who's Invited?

While not yet a common practice in many schools, it is often very helpful to invite your child to all or part of the conference, particularly youngsters past first grade. This is especially true if the conference is not a routine event, but is being held because of a school problem. Certainly, there are times when this would be inappropriate, such as if you are planning to tell the teacher about an impending divorce, details about your child's medical condition, or something else that you wouldn't want to discuss in front of your youngster. But if the problem has to do with academics, homework, or classroom behavior (you can discuss your other private concerns prior to or after the conference), it's best to have the child right there with you and the teacher.

The reason goes back, again, to principles of good communication. It's generally best to have everyone involved in a situation present when it is discussed. Everyone can speak up, ask questions, respectfully disagree, and problem-solve.

If children are not typically included in conferences in your school, let the teacher know beforehand that you'd like to bring your child along to see if she has any objection. Most teachers like the idea once they try it.

When Your Child Has a Different Story

In the more traditional conference between teacher and parent, you might find yourself in a sticky situation. Typically, you go home to discuss with your son what you learned in the conference. To your dismay, your child tells you that the teacher is wrong about whatever she reported to you. The usual excuses run the gamut from "She forgot," "She's lying, I never did that," "She hasn't been feeling well (has been grumpy) and has a poor memory," to "She's gotten me mixed up with the *other* Jonathan!"

There you are, stuck in the middle and not quite sure what to believe. Or perhaps deep down you believe the teacher but, since you have no proof, how do you say this to your son without his feeling that you don't believe him? Also, remember that your child might not be deliberately lying about what he says, but rather may have misperceived the situation.

Once again, having your child attend the conference will prevent this common problem. Typically, the teacher is able to convince both you and the child that the youngster's perception isn't true. If your child is correct (he has calculated his grade accurately and deserves a higher mark), you are there to support him ("I think George averaged those test scores correctly"). If he needs help bringing up his feelings, you can provide a lead ("Honey, why don't you tell Mrs. Smith how you feel about sitting next to Pete?"). With everyone being clear, genuine problem-solving can occur.

THE OLDER ELEMENTARY-SCHOOL CHILD

In some schools, a child leaves the elementary level after completing fifth grade; in others, the end point is sixth grade. Since fifth- and sixth-graders are preadolescents (and some fourth-grade girls have already reached puberty), the older groups will naturally have some different concerns from the youngsters in the earlier grades.

Many older elementary-school students become preoccupied with the body changes that accompany prepuberty and puberty. For the early maturer, self-consciousness about a totally different body (or at least it seems that way!) is likely. The girl who develops breasts, perhaps even beginning her menstrual periods, far ahead of the majority of her classmates may feel as if she's in a different world. Her peers may tease her about her body changes or, worse yet, avoid her altogether.

Even if physical changes have not yet begun, children in fifth and sixth grades vary widely in their level of emotional maturity. Some are playing with dolls and trucks, while others consider such pursuits to be babyish. This second group might be getting interested in the opposite sex, makeup, and boy-girl dances!

Older elementary-school girls often become preoccupied with cliques. Who's "in" and who's "out" becomes a hot topic of conversation, as well as a source of much anguish. The child who must enter a new school in a class made up of cliques can have an especially difficult time.

Peer pressure also becomes more apparent in these older school grades. Kids can become even more sensitive to issues such as fashion, family income, competition, and popularity. They are likely to constantly compare themselves with their peers in order to see how well they measure up both socially and/or academically.

Youngsters in these older grades may also begin to express more annoyance with school, especially if they find schoolwork difficult. Their homework often gets longer and harder, and they sense that the situation will probably worsen with each passing year. The child who has been relying heavily on a parent's help with homework may discover that the parent is no longer able to do the bulk of a child's work for him, either because of the length of the assignments or because the parent might not know (or has forgotten) how to address a particular subject.

OTHER SCHOOL PERSONNEL

If your child has any type of difficulty in school, you'll usually have contact with other personnel besides the teacher. This may include the principal, counselor, a school psychologist, or all of them.

Chapter 9 will deal in greater depth with these problems, as well as with how to work with these personnel. However, the following gives an overview of a parent's possible involvement throughout the school year.

Whom Do You Talk with First?

If you want to bring a concern about your child to the school's attention, it's usually best to discuss the matter with your child's teacher before involving anyone else. Once you've done this (or if you don't feel comfortable talking with the teacher), the next person to contact is usually the counselor. If you've tried unsuccessfully to resolve an issue with your child's teacher, you might choose to go either to the counselor or the principal, depending on your personal preference.

If the problem that concerns you is about school policy, it's usually best to take up the issue directly with the principal. Examples would include a problem with the bus schedule, the dress code, where the children wait before school in the morning, and so on.

If the school calls you because of a problem, it could be that you'll be asked to see the principal or the counselor. If your child has been sent to the principal's office, the principal might want to speak with you first and then might ask you to contact the counselor.

If You Have a Complaint

Present your complaint as objectively as you can, sticking to facts and behaviors rather than interpretations. It helps to make notes beforehand so you don't leave out anything that you want to discuss.

Principals and counselors are much more likely to listen and act on your concern if you present yourself in an organized, calm manner. Remember, you can be forceful and assertive without being aggressive. After your discussion, try to establish a time when you'll be in contact again by phone for feedback about your concern (unless, of course, the situation was resolved in the discussion). It's best to do this so that you'll know when to initiate a call if you don't hear from them. This helps to clarify your expectation, makes the principal or counselor accountable, and allows you not to become a pest by calling unnecessarily.

The Counselor's Role

If your child is having a problem that the counselor might help with, she might talk to your child one or more times. However, remember that her job is to be a troubleshooter and to intervene in a specific situation, not to become your child's therapist. If a problem doesn't get better fairly soon, she might suggest that you consult an outside tutor, speech pathologist, pediatrician, or therapist. She'll probably have a list of public and private resources for you to consider.

The counselor (or principal) might also suggest that there be an intellectual, educational and/or personality evaluation made in order to determine your youngster's current functioning in these areas and his pattern of strengths and weaknesses. If this testing is provided through the school, it will probably be done by a psychologist. Typically, you'll be asked to give your consent for evaluation and then be told whether the psychologist will test your child at the school or at another location.

Once evaluation is completed, a recommendation might be made for your child to receive some special services (special-education classes, speech therapy, and so on). Generally, schools have a meeting time when a child's parents, teacher(s), the counselor, principal, and other school staff meet to make specific recommendations for your child's educational planning. It's very important to be at this meeting if at all possible. Again, you can ask questions, clarify issues, and—most important—voice your opinions about what is being planned. You'll then be asked to sign a consent for whatever plan is to be implemented. (For more information about psychological evaluations and special school meetings concerning your child, see Chapter 9.)

What about the rare situation when all of your efforts to resolve an issue with a school still leave you dissatisfied? If your child is attending a public school, there are a number of measures you can take under the law (see discussion in Chapter 9). Of course, you always have the option to enroll your child in a private or parochial school, or to switch to a different school. Some nonpublic schools have smaller classes and are able to offer a child more individual attention. Some offer a more advanced curriculum for the gifted child. The point is, it's important to be informed about the options you *do* have so that you can effectively act as your child's advocate.

BE HONEST ABOUT YOUR CHILD!

A most important way to be involved in your child's school life is to be open to your child's positive and negative points. Be willing to accept the fact that you might find out that your child has not given you the whole story. If you talk to any school personnel with the attitude that you already know beyond a doubt that your child bears no responsibility for a problem that's occurring, you're likely to alienate everyone involved.

Remember, you want to be your child's advocate, but you don't want to get a reputation as the school pest. If you run interference for every little thing, you'll lose your credibility.

On the other hand, if you have a valid complaint that isn't being addressed, you can sometimes use professionals outside the school system to intervene as consultants. For example, if your child has a learning or psychological problem that is not recognized by the teacher even after you've brought it to her attention, you might have the person who diagnosed the problem give the teacher a call. Most teachers are happy to hear from other professionals who have some insight into a child's classroom problems. If the consultant has a practical suggestion about how the teacher can help the child, the teacher will likely be grateful to have her job made a little easier. If the teacher still disagrees, you can use the professional's opinion to support your position as you talk with other school personnel.

But stay open. You can learn a great deal about your child by listening nondefensively to the perceptions of school personnel.

WHAT'S COMING UP

Now you've got some basics about how to be involved in your child's school, how to establish good rapport with teachers, how to work with school personnel, how to have successful school conferences, and how and when to intervene in your child's behalf. In the chapters that follow, you'll be given some ideas about specific problems your child might encounter in school, and what you as a parent can do to help.

CHAPTER 2

When Your Child Starts School

YOUR CHILD'S VERY FIRST DAY OF SCHOOL IS LIKELY TO BE A momentous event, for you as well as for your youngster. The "big day" is usually met with great anticipation and a sense of excitement.

Even if this is not your child's first year in school, the beginning of *any* new school year is usually thought of as a "fresh start." After all, the event marks the beginning of much more than just a school experience. It's also a time for setting up a new routine. Vacation time is over, and it's time to get back to a regular (or at least new) schedule. This can include changing the time for waking up, eating meals, and going to bed at night. There may be a new car pool, bus, or other transportation arrangement to get used to, new playtime rules, and new after-school care arrangements. And of course, let's not forget the importance of setting aside time for homework. All of this not only means that your *child* has to get used to a new routine, but that *you* have to, as well!

To reduce stress on the whole family, it's wise to understand the anxieties that may surface for you and for your child at this important time, and for everyone to be prepared for the changes to come. A little thought given to these matters in advance of the "big day" will make it easier for everyone.

WHAT IS EVERYONE SO WORRIED ABOUT?

Underneath all the hoopla about starting school, both you and your child are likely to be having some unsettling thoughts. As with any fear, it's best to ask "What's the worst that could happen?" and get the concern out in the open.

Common Worries About Your Child

So what are the common fears that you might have about your youngster's entering this new phase of her life? As you think about it, you'll realize that your child is now going to be evaluated and compared with other children her age. This fact, in itself, is enough to set your worry wheels spinning!

You might think your child is brilliant, charming, and wonderful, but what will her teacher think? What if she doesn't measure up to your expectations intellectually? What if she doesn't do well on tests?

What if the other children make fun of her? What if she's timid, quiet, or sensitive? What if she tends to have a temper or acts too aggressive? What if she's been raised to be a "free spirit" and balks at the structure of school?

What if your child gets a no-nonsense teacher, when she needs one who's very warm and nurturing? What if she needs lots of structure, but the teacher wants her students to be independent self-starters?

What if your child has some physical or learning difference which will set her apart from the other children? What if your child has experienced a traumatic family situation (death, divorce, and so on) and is in a difficult adjustment period?

Although your fears could stem from legitimate concerns presented by your *child's* behavior, abilities, or circumstances, realize that there may be other factors at work. You might be worried simply because of your own insecurities about your ability to measure up as a parent. Or, on closer analysis, you might find that your worries come out of your *own* past experiences in school. If so, it's quite normal that you would want to spare your child any experience that was uncomfortable or frightening for you. Just realizing that your fears about your child are projections from your own past can be reassuring.

Whatever the source of your worries, it's likely that you'll face your child's going to school with a mixture of anticipation and specific concerns. You'll find some helpful hints throughout this book on how to handle the possible school-related problems that could occur. In the meantime, emphasize the positives about school to your child, and forgive yourself for having normal parental anxiety!

More Personal Worries

If this is your child's first time to go to "real school" (not just nursery or preschool), you could find yourself having pangs of sadness. After all, this time is a landmark. It means that your youngster is leaving the more protected world of toddlerhood and entering the world of childhood. This fact, in itself, can make you nostalgic about those "baby days." You might even have thoughts like "Have I given my best to my child during her critical early years?" or "Have I laid a solid foundation for my child's emotional growth?"

If you've stayed home with your child during his preschool years, you might worry how he will fare without you around so much of the time. Sometimes, of course, you wonder how you'll fare without him!

If this is your first child, you could be filled with thoughts of potentially awful things that might happen to him out in that "real world" of school. If it's your last child, you could be suddenly struck with the realization that you don't have a baby at home anymore. If you've been staying home with your child, your proclamations to your friends about finally getting your "freedom" may ring empty in your ears as you suddenly feel at a loss about what to do with all that "free" time. You might even begin to feel "not needed."

Sometimes problems in your marital relationship that have been lying dormant can suddenly surface as less of your time is required for taking care of a child. Or you may feel bored with your life. So this can be a time when you find yourself rethinking your options about further education, career goals, and/or your relationship.

These kinds of feelings are common to parents who are getting ready to send a child to school. Just as your child is entering a transition, so too are you. Simply notice how you feel, rather than deny it, and move on. Most of all, remember to be gentle with yourself.

Worries Your Child Might Have

No matter how enthusiastically you might try to convince your child that a new school year will be a wonderful adventure, your youngster is still likely to have some worries of her own. Her concerns are likely to be quite specific and concrete. Typical examples might include:

- What if I can't find the bathroom?
- Will my teacher like me?
- Will the bigger kids pick on me?
- What if I get lost trying to find my classroom?
- What if Mom/Dad isn't there to pick me up after school?
- What if I get sick in class?
- What if I break my pencil and I can't find another one?
- What if I have an accident in my pants?
- What if I don't know anyone else in the class?
- What will my parents do if I don't make good grades?
- What if I can't keep up with everybody?
- What if I'm not as smart as the other kids?
- What if the other kids make fun of me?
- What if I have to read out loud and I can't?
- What if my teacher is mean?

While your child might voice his fears aloud, he also might not. Don't assume that he has no worries just because he doesn't verbalize them to you. You might encourage him to confide in you by saying something like "Honey, lots of times kids have some worries about school, but they feel kind of silly talking about them.

No worry is silly, though. Is there anything that you are worried about?"

This conversation gives your child the permission he might need to open up to you about his concerns. If he does, you can give him appropriate reassurance. Role playing with puppets can also be helpful, both in eliciting your child's fears as well as in showing him through play how to deal with them.

PREPARING YOUR CHILD TO START SCHOOL

Getting your child ready to begin school involves more than just talking about school itself. It also includes selecting the kinds of clothes your child will wear to school, as well as establishing guidelines for a new daily routine.

Getting Your Child Familiar with a New School

Whether it's your child's very first time to go to a school, or the first time in a new school, he'll feel more comfortable if he knows what to expect. This is why many kindergarten and elementary schools have an "orientation" in the summer before school begins. Parents and children use this time to become familiar with the general layout of the school, including the principal's office, the gym, the nurse's office, the bathrooms, the library/learning center, the water fountains, the cafeteria, and the playground. Most important, each child and her parents are given an opportunity to meet the child's teacher and to visit the classroom. This is certainly an ideal way to get both parents and children comfortable with a new school.

But not every school has such a program, or perhaps your new school does, but you cannot attend for some reason. Check with the school to see if it will be open a few days before classes begin, and ask if you and your child can visit at that time. If not, you can at least take your child to the school playground and show him the building. Take him up to the front entrance, look in a few windows (if you can), and show him where you will be picking him up at the end of the day.

If you don't get an opportunity to meet your child's teacher until the first day of school, but you know the teacher's name, it might be possible to ask parents in the neighborhood about what the teacher looks like, or any special characteristic about her or her classroom that your child would find interesting or exciting. Even if all a child knows is that his teacher has long red hair and has two hamsters in her room, this information helps to reduce his fear of the unknown.

Selecting School Clothes

Unless you want to risk setting yourself up for morning battles with your child about clothing, make your child's comfort a top priority when you select school apparel. Your youngster may have idiosyncrasies about certain materials being "scratchy," not liking buttons or zippers, or not having elastic around the waist or on sleeves. She may complain that some clothing styles are too tight, too loose, or too *something*.

And then there's the matter of style and color. Some girls want to wear dresses or skirts; some hate them. Boys also have specific preferences about the kind of clothes they wear. The point is, that little plaid outfit with the cat on the pocket that you find so adorable may bring nothing but scowls from the one who has to wear it!

Certainly, you'll establish the rules about appropriateness of certain apparel. You don't want your child wearing to school the fancy church outfit that Grandmother gave her. You'll also have rules about what is appropriate depending on the weather. A superhero tank top and shorts just won't cut it when it's freezing outside!

But within the limits provided by the school dress code and matters of appropriateness, a wise parent will not push a certain kind of clothing on a child who has a definite aversion to it. While you don't want to allow your daughter to manipulate you into granting her every whim, you do want to give her the healthy message that she is an individual, and that you take her preferences into account. In addition, encouraging her to select her clothes for school increases her growing independence. Besides, it's simply not worth the hassle to get into a power struggle with your child about her clothes.

So let comfort and convenience be your guide. Select clothes that your child can easily put on and get off. Buy shoes with soles that allow her to run and play without having to worry about slipping or falling. If she has trouble tying shoelaces, look for shoes with Velcro closures.

It's also wise to check out what's *"in"* according to standards of dress at your child's school. For example, in many schools, the length of a girl's skirt is critical. If you make your daughter wear a skirt that comes below her knees, when her peers all wear them above, you'll be setting her up for ridicule.

Establishing the New Routine

The start of school is welcomed by many parents as a "fresh start" for them to reestablish (or establish) family routines. In many households, the rules for the children's getting up in the morning, eating meals, playing outside, and going to bed have loosened a bit over the summer.

Now it's necessary to make sure your child has time for school itself, for homework, and for a home life. He may be involved in a sport that will be starting up for the year, as well as other nonschool classes (piano, gymnastics, and so on). But he still needs time to eat, to sleep, to play with his friends, to do chores, and to spend time just hanging out with the family.

Getting Up in the Morning

Be sure to allow enough time in the morning for your child to get dressed and eat breakfast without having to rush. Children, like adults, have different biological rhythms. If your son tends to move slowly by nature (as opposed to the youngster who dawdles as part of a power struggle over getting dressed), you'll avoid a lot of hassle by waking him up earlier. Also have him gather together his clothes and school supplies the night before.

Homework Time

Typically, first-grade teachers will ask parents to spend ten or fifteen minutes daily working with a child on some type of reading or math skill. As the child gets older, the likelihood increases that he'll have formal homework assignments. Even if your child's teacher does not assign homework, it's helpful to get your youngster into the habit of reading a little each evening. So be sure to work this time into your child's schedule. (For more about homework, see Chapter 7.)

Sports and Lessons

While it's wonderful to provide your child with opportunities to play a sport or learn a skill, many families find that they can quickly become overwhelmed as their children become over-scheduled. A good rule of thumb is to allow your child to participate in only one "extracurricular" activity at a time, especially if the activity you choose involves more than a once-a-week commitment. Remember that you can give your youngster exposure to many different activities throughout grade school by allowing her to try something different each semester or year. While a child should generally finish a commitment to a particular activity (a set series of lessons, one season's sport, lessons for one semester), she needs the option to try something else.

Chores

Children who are required to do age-appropriate chores around the house are likely to be better organized in school. The child who can't find his math paper because it was crumpled in the back pocket of his jeans and fell out on the playground is often a child who is not required to take responsibility at home. As much as they complain about chores, kids tend to feel better about themselves when they know they're helpful. Even a child in kindergarten can pick up her toys, bring her dishes from the table to the sink, water plants, or perform other simple tasks. As she gets older, increase the complexity of what's required.

Play

In an effort to get a child to focus on homework or other "constructive" activities after school, a parent may be dismayed when the child balks, saying, "But I want to PLAY!" What that well-intentioned parent doesn't understand is that school is work for a child. After being expected to comply with a set schedule all day (often with little choice about what to do), kids need to unwind. In play they can blow off steam, move about as they wish, and freely choose their activities.

Also, play is much more than just idle leisure for children. Play expands their creativity and teaches them how to occupy themselves without external entertainment. Play also provides the opportunity for youngsters to work through their fears and anxieties. For example, a child who has to have surgery might play "hospital" before the surgery is scheduled as well as for weeks after the surgery is over.

Family Time

With today's busy lifestyles, it's easy to overlook the time a family needs just to be together. This means time to goof off, to watch a television program, to play a game, to go on an outing, to get caught up in a lively discussion about a topic, to play with pets, and so on. To have that kind of spontaneity, there simply has to be time for it to occur. Time can become a precious commodity during the school year, especially when homework is assigned.

One of the most common ways to insure at least *some* family time is for the entire family to eat at least one meal together every day. While this point might seem obvious, it's amazing how many families allow everyone to fix their own food when they want it or to eat in shifts, even when everyone is at home. In other families, television is the main object of attraction at meals, preventing spontaneous conversation. By developing a regular habit of everyone eating together whenever possible (or at least sitting at the table, even if choosing not to eat) and having no other distractions, you'll be ensuring that you have at least a minimum of quality family time.

Bedtime

It's wise to establish a set bedtime for children in kindergarten and elementary school, whether or not school is in session. This procedure not only ensures that the child gets proper rest, but also that a parent has "grown-up time" for herself and/or for her mate. When children stay up until the parents go to bed, parents eventually find that they have no time for themselves or for their relationship as a couple. Whether married or single, this takes a huge emotional toll and can easily create feelings of hopelessness, resentment, and/or depression in the couple and/or the individual.

When a child starts going to school as a kindergartener, set a fairly early bedtime if possible (around seven-thirty or eight o'clock). Let him know that as he gets older, his bedtime will be later. This plan allows a parent to give a youngster the privilege of staying up later as he gets older, but ensures that he'll still have a reasonable bedtime (around nine o'clock) when he gets to fourth and fifth grade.

But what if you have one of those children who doesn't require much sleep? You can still insist that a youngster go to bed at a reasonable time. Tell her that she doesn't have to go to sleep, but she does have to stay in bed and have "quiet time" before she does fall asleep. Quite often, you'll find that once you become firm on this, she'll fall asleep fairly soon after going to bed.

If after trying this plan out for a week or so, you find that your child is still awake more than thirty to forty-five minutes after he goes to bed (with lights off, and without coming out of his room), you might allow him to keep his light on and read for a certain time period (but not to get out of bed and play), or to keep the lights off but to listen to cassette tapes (*calming* stories or music) or to the radio until the time he'll normally fall asleep.

COMMON PROBLEM SITUATIONS

READY FOR FIRST GRADE?

You just had the routine end-of-year conference with Tommy's kindergarten teacher. To your complete surprise, she recommended that you consider holding Tommy back a year to let him repeat kindergarten. You're not at all sure that she's right. What should you do?

If you could gather together a group of children who were all having their sixth birthday on that day, you would quickly notice big differences in their levels of maturity. Turning six doesn't automatically mean that a child is ready for first grade. If Tommy had sailed smoothly through kindergarten, keeping up with the work and socializing appropriately, there would probably be no question that he could handle first grade the next year. The kindergarten teacher in all likelihood would have given him her blessings, and confidently put him on the first-grade roster.

But what if your son is in that borderline zone, handling some areas of kindergarten easily, but struggling with others? Perhaps he has difficulty executing kindergarten tasks (recognizing letters, elementary counting, producing a simple drawing that is above the scribbling level, and so on). Maybe he *can* do the tasks, but has great difficulty controlling his behavior (aggressive to other children, won't play cooperatively, is unable or unwilling to comply with a teacher's simple requests, and so on). It may be that he doesn't participate with the class, quietly "doing his own thing" while the other children are involved in group activities. Or, he might still be quite dependent on adults to do things for him, requesting constant individual help with most tasks or activities.

Any one of these factors is a "red flag." This means that you need to take a close look at the question of whether or not it might be wise to hold your child back a year.

Some Comforting News

Put aside all ideas that your child has somehow "failed" (or that you have failed as a parent!) if the question of first-grade placement arises. What is considered to be "normal" development of five- and six-year-olds includes a very wide range of capabilities and behaviors. The possibility that your child would be better off waiting another year for first grade does *not* mean that he's not smart, that he's not going to achieve well in school, or even that he has any kind of learning problem.

Also, realize that there are definite advantages to having your child start first grade at age seven. If you push a child on because you think he "can do it," you might be right. But the question is, how *easily* can he do it? If he is able to keep up with first grade, but only with lots of extra effort, he's likely to struggle along at the *lower* end of his class. If he waits another year to mature, he might well be in the *top* range of his class, without struggle. And not only might he be in the top academically, but he's likely to have an advantage over his classmates in athletics as well. What could be better for your child than to feel competent and successful?

How Do You Decide What to Do?

Your child's kindergarten teacher is your first resource for making this important decision. Remember, she has had a class full of youngsters with whom to compare your child (and maybe many classes before this one). Few parents have such experience with large numbers of five- and six-year olds. Take her recommendation seriously, ask her any questions you might have about your child's readiness for first grade, and listen carefully to what she says.

In addition, many public and private schools perform "readiness" testing for first grade near the end of the kindergarten year. While not a full-scale educational evaluation, these tests very often give useful information about your child's strengths and weaknesses regarding school tasks. If your kindergartener has his sixth birthday in the late spring or summer, shortly before the first-grade year begins, there is a higher probability that his maturity level will be significantly lower than the children who turned six *earlier* in their kindergarten year. The child who is less mature than most of his classmates is likely to be very frustrated with the demands of first grade.

If you disagree with the teacher's recommendations, just want a second opinion, or find yourself confused and unsure about what to do, arrange to have your child receive a full educational evaluation. It's very hard to be objective about your own offspring, and you might question the teacher's objectivity also. A qualified professional will give you feedback from the evaluation, and can help you put the parts of the academic/social/emotional puzzle together to make the best decision for your child. (For more about educational testing, see Chapter 9.)

An additional option is to enroll your child in a summer tutoring program run by educational specialists. These professionals can work with your child on strengthening his weaknesses, and are in an excellent position at the end of the summer to make a fully informed recommendation about whether or not you should send your child on to first grade.

Is There a "Right" Class for the Kindergarten Repeater?

Obviously, you won't want your child to feel that he's repeating the same class he already had. That means that you'll want a different teacher. Some parents even choose to enroll their child in a kindergarten in a different school, perhaps returning to the original school the following year.

If your child had difficulty both academically and socially with kindergarten, it's fine for him to attend a class where most of the children are first-timers in kindergarten. But if he did well on some kindergarten tasks, try to enroll him in a class in which all of the children are second-year kindergarten students. Many times, these classes are called "transitional first grades," and the teachers have special training in working with children of this age. These teachers will often individualize the curriculum so that a child will get first-grade work in the areas where he is ready for it, but will also be given special help in beefing up his areas of weakness.

HOW DO YOU TELL A CHILD SHE NEEDS TO REPEAT KINDERGARTEN?

You feel very strongly that Samantha is just not ready for first grade. But how do you tell her that she's going back to kindergarten?

Many parents worry that a decision to have their child repeat kindergarten will be traumatic for the youngster and will negatively influence her self-esteem. The fact is that when a youngster does feel upset about repeating kindergarten past the first week or so of the new school year, it's usually a clue that the child's *parents* are upset, embarrassed, or otherwise having problems with the decision! Most children generally accept this situation, so long as it is presented to them in a positive way.

If your daughter has a "late" birthday, there's a very easy way to present your decision not to have her go to first grade. You can say something like "Samantha, many children who have summer birthdays don't start first grade until they're seven. Dad and I think that's the best thing for you, too."

But what if your child's birthday is earlier in the year? You could tell her, "Samantha, lots of kids go to first grade when they are seven instead of six. It's better, because school is easier for them by having that extra year to grow up. Besides, it's nice to be one of the older kids in your class; you know how younger kids look up to older ones."

Or you might handle it this way: "Samantha, some of the work in kindergarten was a little hard for you (give examples). By working on those things next year in kindergarten, you'll be much happier and find the work a lot easier when you go to first grade. Besides, kids begin first grade either at six or at seven, and I think it will be best for you to start at seven."

If these comments are delivered matter-of-factly, your child won't be left with the impression that you are angry or dissatisfied with her. What she may be concerned about, however, is that many of her friends from kindergarten will be going on to first grade. Reassure her that she can still ask those children over and be friends with them, but that she'll also make new friends in her new class. Once school starts and a week or two have gone by, she'll have new friends to replace any who might not keep in contact with her. A really close neighborhood friend whom she plays with often will probably still remain a good friend.

Although you'll be positive and upbeat with your daughter about your decision to have her delay first grade, you still want to encourage her to discuss any feelings she has about this decision. Ask her, "Honey, how do you feel about not going to first grade next year?" Watch for any signals that she thinks she's "dumb," or is worried that the other kids will think so. If you pick up on this, reassure her that the decision has nothing to do with her not being smart, and that many very smart, successful adults went to first grade when they were seven. If she worries that other kids will think she's stupid, let her know that those children just don't understand the facts, and that many kids just enjoy finding any excuse to tease someone. (For more about helping your child handle teasing, see Chapter 4.)

NOT WANTING TO BE LEFT AT SCHOOL

You've done a good job preparing Jennifer for school, and she is very excited as the two of you set off for her "first day." But when it's time for you to leave her in the classroom, she looks terrified, cries, holds on to you for dear life, and begs you not to leave her.

For the child who has basically stayed at home most days with a parent, housekeeper, or sitter, those first days of being left at school can be traumatic. Even youngsters who have been accustomed to going to nursery or preschool for several hours a day can balk about being left for the much longer school day.

For this reason, many kindergarten teachers will invite both parent and child into the classroom for a brief period, perhaps half an hour or so. This gives the child a chance to get used to the teacher and classroom, and to get involved in some activity before the parent leaves. This policy usually lasts a couple of weeks, and is an ideal way to help a child deal with the transition of starting to spend six or seven hours a day at school.

Whether or not a parent is invited into the classroom, some children still do not accept the fact that a parent must eventually leave them at school. Typically, such a child will cling to a parent, crying or screaming, as the parent tries to make a graceful exit. This kind of behavior is labeled a separation problem.

However, just because a youngster has been to kindergarten does not mean that she might not show separation problems in the first, or even later, grades. Some first-graders who went through kindergarten without a qualm will suddenly balk about being left at school that first day. If this situation occurs with your first-grader, request that you be given a little visitation time in the classroom for a few days (since this usually is a policy only in kindergarten).

For the older elementary-school child who develops a separation problem, see Chapter 8 for more suggestions.

Managing a Separation Problem

It can be very unsettling for a parent to turn and walk away from a bawling, out-of-control child who's perhaps pleading "Mommy! Don't leave me!" between sobs. Even the most rational parent is likely to feel guilty, wondering if she should have perhaps stayed a little longer with the child, or if she has done something terribly wrong in her parenting.

As difficult as it is, the best thing a parent can do is to stay matter-of-fact and upbeat, giving the child a parting hug and reminding him of who will pick him up at the end of the school day. If necessary, the child may have to be gently but swiftly pried away from the parent and given over to the teacher.

Remember that the teacher has no doubt seen this behavior many times before, and is prepared to deal with it. As experienced kindergarten teachers will tell you, most seemingly hysterical children will calm down within a few minutes of the parent's departure. But the parent who lingers, trying to plead, bribe, or reason with the child, only encourages the child to protest more.

By being firm when it's time to leave, you are telling your child with your *behavior* what you've been saying in words—that he's safe. By lingering, getting upset yourself, and apologizing for having to leave, you are unwittingly sending the message that there really *might* be something to fear.

Does the Parent Have a Separation Problem?

While most parents insist that they want their child to go off happily to school, some parents unconsciously may have the opposite wish. Such a parent might be lonely or frightened about being alone. She might be overly anxious that something bad will happen to her child, either because of some experience with tragedy in the past or because she feels guilty and expects to be punished.

She might fear the loss of control over a child that comes with the child's growing up and becoming exposed to the world. Or she may overly identify with her child, wanting to experience his every action. Again, such feelings are usually not conscious to the person who is experiencing them.

If your child cannot be consoled at school for hours after you've left, or if he continues to have trouble separating from you after the first couple weeks of school, you might do some soul-searching to see if you are the one having the problem. If you think this possibility exists, psychotherapy with a mental health professional can be very helpful.

THE CHILD WHO DISLIKES SCHOOL
THE FIRST DAY

Brandon is eager to start second grade and has no problem when you leave him in the classroom that first day. But you find him in a very different frame of mind when you pick him up later that afternoon. To your dismay, he announces, "I hate school and I never want to go back!"

Instead of jumping right in and telling Brandon that he *has* to go to school, or giving him a pep talk about how he will learn to like school, simply reflect back his frustration and *listen*. You might say something like "Gee, honey, sounds like you had a pretty awful day. What happened?"

Continue reflecting back his feelings as he talks about what happened during the day. For example: "So you got really scared when you saw the fifth-graders"; "So you were really angry when that boy broke your pencil"; "So the boy hurt your feelings when he called you names"; "So you think the teacher doesn't like you because she didn't smile at you"; and so on.

After you think you've gotten the full story, ask your son what ideas he might have for improving the situation. He just might come up with a good idea, once he's talked through the problem. If he does, you have the chance to praise him for his good thinking.

If your child is too overwhelmed to think of anything to improve the situation, it's time to give him your ideas. This could be anything from telling him, "We'll go to school early tomorrow and figure out where the bathroom is that's closest to your classroom," to giving him tips on dealing with name-calling. If the problem is one that you think your son cannot handle by himself, you might tell him that you'll send a note to his teacher the next day to let her know about the problem.

Be alert to the possibility that your child's strong negative reaction to that first day may have nothing to do with school itself. Perhaps he's having a problem with being away from you, or from his familiar surroundings. Maybe he's feeling jealous of a younger sibling who gets to stay home and have the benefit of your total attention.

If you suspect that this is the case, he'll need a little extra attention from you for a while. Reassure him that you and he will have your "special time" together each day. This will be a set time every day (about ten or fifteen minutes) in which you will devote your total attention to him. During that time, *he* can direct the activity (within reason!). For instance, he might choose to have you play a game with him, rub his back, play with his hamster, color together, sing to him, or rock him. By having the reassurance that you and he will have this "special time," he'll be better able to go off to school without feeling deprived of your attention.

It's also possible that your child has a temperament that has been labeled "slow to warm up." Such children experience anxiety whenever there's a change in their environment (moving, new school), or when they begin something new (a new school year, swimming lessons). Even if it's something they've been looking forward to, their first reaction once they begin is to want to quit. However, when given a few weeks to adjust, they adapt beautifully.

If you have a slow-to-warm-up child, help him understand his own temperament. Let him know that he usually feels scared whenever he begins something new, but that he does just fine after a short time. Remind him of some occasions in the past when he wanted to quit some activity or situation, but then ended up loving it.

No matter how much your child might protest, you want to be gently firm about the matter of his going to school. Resist the temptation to keep him home a few days so he'll be less upset, as this almost always makes things worse. (For more information on helping a child who continues to refuse to go to school, see Chapter 8.)

As you listen to and talk with your child, remain calm and matter-of-fact. This attitude conveys the message that the problem is certainly fixable, and models a healthy problem-solving approach to life's problems.

For the older child who says he's never going back to school, see Chapter 8.

WHAT HAPPENED TO ALL THE TOYS?

When you pick up Jason from his first day in second grade, you can see that he's upset. When you ask him what's wrong, he replies, "There aren't any *toys* in our classroom!"

Whether it's first grade or a later one, the day will come when your child will go to a classroom and find that it looks like "real school." Gone are all the toys he's been used to in preschool and kindergarten.

While you want to let your son know that school does include some fun activities, beware of setting him up for disappointment by making grade school sound like it's all fun and games. Prepare him by letting him know what a typical grade-school classroom looks like. Let him know that going to school is the kid's equivalent of a grown-up's going to work. The primary purpose is learning, not entertainment or play.

Reassure him, of course, that he'll have plenty of time for play and for toys when he's not in school. It isn't that he has to give up these activities, but that school is the appropriate place for learning about his world and for developing skills that will help him as he grows up.

THE CONFINEMENT OF SCHOOL

Melissa arrives home from school complaining that her teacher asked her to sit at a desk most of the day. You know that your daughter is the kind of youngster who has a high activity level and who hates to sit in one place for too long. How do you help her cope with the confinement of a typical classroom?

While many teachers understand that some children actually learn better when they can move around, and many even design their classrooms to allow for this, other teachers still prefer the more traditional sit-at-your-desk policy. If your daughter has difficulty following a policy of sitting quietly at a desk for classroom activities, acknowledge that you understand that it's hard for her. Encourage her to take full advantage of any times in the school routine when she *can* move around without getting into trouble. You might include these suggestions:

- Volunteer to clean the blackboard, or to pass items to other students when the teacher asks for someone to distribute materials.
- Be as physically active as possible during appropriate times, such as in physical education class or during recess.
- Take bathroom and drink breaks whenever they are allowed, even if you don't need to.
- Volunteer to run errands to the school office or to other classrooms whenever these opportunities present themselves.

It can also help to teach your child a way that she can make *subtle, minor* muscle movements that will not be distracting to other students and will be acceptable to the teacher. This includes wiggling her toes inside her shoes, feeling a comforting item that is worn around her neck (a medallion, stone, arrowhead, and so on), tapping her fingers on the desk or on her leg *without making any sound,* and so on.

Youngsters can also be taught to develop a special personal signal to themselves (technically called an "anchor") which they can use whenever they need to be in a calm, resourceful learning state. This procedure is easier to learn by watching a demonstration than by reading about it, but if you'll hang in there while I describe how to teach your child this process, you can give him a wonderful tool that will greatly assist him in school.

Teaching Your Child an "Anchor"

Ask your child to recall a time when he was able to sit quietly and concentrate his full attention while something was being taught to him. The occasion he selects could be a time when he was listening to a coach, learning something from television, reading an interesting book, putting together a puzzle, watching his father build a model car—any time when he was focusing his attention and sitting quietly.

Next, decide on the signal that will become your child's anchor. A kinesthetic, or touch, anchor works well. Common ones include pressing his thumb to the end of his first finger with his nondominant hand (so he can still write while using the anchor), making a quick fist movement, or squeezing the palm of one hand with the other hand.

He can also combine one of these kinesthetic anchors with a visual and/or auditory anchor. For example, a visual anchor might be *imagining* a spaceship over his head "beaming down" his favorite calming color. The auditory anchor would be *saying* to himself the name of the color he chose, or any related word (such as "blue," "beam," or "calm"). By inviting a child to use an anchor that includes kinesthetic, visual, and auditory sensory channels, you will maximize your child's success in developing a succesful anchor (for more about sensory channels, see Chapter 9).

Now that you've gotten your child to think of a *learning situation* when he was able to absorb something easily and with full attention, and you've developed the anchor he will use, you're ready to set the anchor. Ask him to close his eyes, take a few deep breaths, relax his body, and think of a *quiet place* where he could be happy and calm (lying on a raft in a swimming pool or river, lying on a beach listening to the ocean, floating on his favorite-color cloud, getting a back rub, etc.). When you see that he is relaxed, ask him to imagine the *learning situation* he'd selected and remember how easily he'd been able to pay attention and to learn what was being taught. Make sure he mentally puts himself right into the situation *as if he's actually there* (not like he's *watching* himself in the scene as if seeing himself on a movie screen).

When you are clear that your child is mentally in the learning situation, ask him to use the anchors you've established. Tell him that these anchors will trigger his brain to remember the calm, attentive learning state whenever he needs to use them. Then ask him to come back to his normal alert state and report his experience. If he says he had trouble with any part of the exercise, repeat it until he is able to feel good about it.

After your son reports a successful experience with this visualization process, ask him to close his eyes, imagine himself in school the next day when the teacher is beginning to explain something, and then again fire his anchor. Have him open his eyes and tell you how he felt when he saw himself using his anchor in class. Continue working at this process until your child learns to associate the anchor with the resourceful, calm learning state.

You can also instruct your son to establish a "classroom anchor" for himself. Let him pick some item or sound in his classroom (such as the flag, a teacher's desk, the ringing bell, and so on) and, when he's in the relaxed state described above, ask him to imagine the item or sound and to use it in the future to trigger his resourceful learning state.

Instruct your child that he can use any one (or all) of his anchors whenever he wants to prepare himself to settle down and concentrate. Let him know that the procedure has helped to train his brain to put him immediately into a state where he can relax, concentrate, and be ready to learn. Children usually love these anchors and enjoy having them handy whenever they need to settle down and concentrate.

REFUSING TO TALK ABOUT SCHOOL

You can't wait to pick up Richard from school and hear all about his very first day. To your dismay, your eager efforts to draw him out result only in frustrating responses like "Fine," "It was okay," or a shoulder shrug!

Although your enthusiasm to hear about your child's day at school is understandable, realize that many youngsters simply don't like to discuss school. It might be that your child is not very talkative in general. Or it could be that he feels he's had enough of having to answer questions for one day, especially when he first sees you after school.

While your enthusiasm and curiosity might lead you to push him for answers, this tactic will in all likelihood just make him clam up further. It's best to bide your time, let him unwind, and wait for him to be in a more conversational mood.

Instead of mentally tearing your hair about his lack of communication, try asking a more specific question. You might ask what he played during recess, what he read that day in language arts, what kind of math he studied that day, how the classroom pets are doing, and so on. Sometimes a child will respond to a request to tell a parent "something good" or "something funny" that happened during the day.

There can be a fine line between encouraging your child to talk, versus sounding like an interrogator! If your son rejects your first couple of attempts to get him to talk, drop the subject without further comment. Some kids simply need time to wind down from the day's activities, are more interested in getting to the refrigerator to find a snack, or are eager to get outside to play. Be sensitive to the times your child is more receptive to conversation (while he's eating, just before bed, during reading time, and so on) rather than pressuring him to talk on your timetable. Resist the temptation to lecture him on his not talking to you about school (a sure way to get him to clam up). Your patience will usually pay off.

A CLASS FULL OF STRANGERS

Eric comes home from his first day at school with a dejected look. He says he doesn't know any of the other children in his class, and tearfully announces that he doesn't have any friends.

Admit to your child that you understand how hard it is not to know anyone in class. After all, everyone likes to see a familiar face in a new situation.

Then, point out to him other times in the past when he met a new child or group of children. Remind him of how quickly he and the other youngster(s) got to know one another.

Although many of his classmates might already be acquainted with other children in the room, chances are good that there's at least one other child who is in the same situation as your child. Suggest that your son look for a child in the room who also seems not to know anyone, and attempt to befriend that child.

You could also send a brief note to school to alert the teacher that your child is upset about not knowing anyone in the class. Teachers can work wonders in such situations, setting up tasks in such a manner that children are paired with others who are also in need of a friend.

Reassure your child that what he needs is, simply, a little time. Encourage him to be friendly to his classmates, and let nature take its course. (For more about helping your child make friends, see Chapter 4.)

CHANGING SCHOOLS IN MIDYEAR

You've just found out that you are moving to another city in the middle of Amy's third-grade year. Aside from preparing her for the new school, is there anything you need to do to help her leave the old school?

Many youngsters find themselves needing to change schools before the end of the year, for various reasons. Parents are usually pretty good about preparing them for the physical change to a new school. (For information on preparing a child for handling the *social* aspects of changing schools in midyear, see Chapter 4.) What they often forget, however, is to allow the child to say her good-byes to the teacher and children she will be leaving behind.

Even though you think your daughter might cry or be sad as she says these good-byes, know that it's perfectly normal and even healthy for her to react in this way. Give her support in such a situation, and let her know that it's important for her to acknowledge her sadness.

Also, give your daughter an address book before her last day at the old school, and let her collect the addresses of her teacher and special friends she might want to write to after she gets to her new location. Even though you think she might not follow through with sending letters to her old classmates, just knowing that she has a way to contact them will be reassuring to her. Also, she could take a scrapbook to school the last day, asking her friends to draw a picture and/or write her a message as a keepsake.

CHAPTER 3

Teacher Troubles

WHEN THE MATCH BETWEEN YOUR CHILD AND HIS TEACHER IS A good one, you can count yourself lucky and breathe a sigh of relief. After all, a child's teacher has tremendous impact on a youngster's attitudes toward school and toward learning in general.

When a child has difficulty relating to his teacher, or the teacher has a wrong impression about the child, the school year can easily become more negative than positive. Since most children stay in their originally assigned classrooms throughout the entire school year, it's vitally important to iron out any difficulties as they surface.

To complicate matters even more, youngsters typically will start out comparing their current teacher with the one they had the year before. If your son loved his last teacher, the new one may have a hard act to follow. Also, rumors about teachers spread quickly from one child to another. Sometimes a youngster makes up his mind about whether a teacher is "good" or "bad" because of something another child has said about her, even before the child has had personal experience with her. Because of these two factors, teachers often have hurdles to jump with their students—and with their students' parents—right from the very first day of class.

A PARENT'S BIAS

Let's face it. It's hard to be a parent and *not* be a little biased toward your child! Also, parents hear rumors about teachers that sometimes make those parents worry about the teacher to whom their child is assigned. So when your youngster tells you something about a teacher that seems negative, you're naturally going to want to believe him.

But common sense will tell you that your child's perception might not be accurate. Besides, there are usually two believable sides to every story.

However, it's just as unfair to assume immediately that your child is misperceiving a situation as it is to think automatically that he's correct. While you don't want naively to swallow everything he says, you also don't want him to feel that you are unsupportive of him. So how do you strike this delicate balance?

When your child complains about a teacher, you can sympathetically reflect back his *feelings* about the situation without agreeing or disagreeing with him. For example, if your son complains that the teacher refuses to call on him when he raises his hand, you might say something like "It must be really confusing not to understand why she doesn't call on you."

After you've helped your child feel understood, ask him what ideas he has about why the problem is occurring. In the same example, you might try, "Well, what do you think might be the reason she's not calling on you?" After hearing him out, give him some alternative ideas he hasn't thought of, if appropriate.

Next, ask your son if he has any ideas about what he could do to help the situation. By asking him for solutions before offering your own, you're helping him to learn to problem-solve.

If, after hearing your child's story, you aren't clear about exactly what is going on, let him know that you are confused. On the one hand, you can see how he feels, based on his interpretation of the situation; on the other hand, you need a little more information in order to get a better handle on the problem.

If your child is willing and able to check things out further with his teacher, encourage him to do so and report back to you. If your child is too young or too shy to get the necessary information for you, or if the matter seems quite serious, let your child know that you'll be sending the teacher a note or talking with her by phone to discuss the matter. Of course, there's always the option of requesting a joint meeting between the teacher, your child, and yourself.

COMMON PROBLEM SITUATIONS

THE TEACHER YELLS

Tammy arrives home from school one day with a dejected look. When you ask what's wrong, she tells you that her teacher yells at her.

Some people talk louder than others, and teachers are no exception. In fact, teachers sometimes have to talk somewhat forcefully to make a point in a noisy classroom. When this happens, some youngsters will complain that the teacher is yelling when, in fact, she's really not.

Such a complaint might come from a child who lives in a very quiet family, where the adults rarely raise their voices. On the other hand, some youngsters are frightened by loudness because there is a high level of yelling and/or aggression in their homes. There are also children who are very sensitive and who interpret everything that a teacher says in a loud voice as a personal criticism.

Help your child understand that there's a difference between talking loudly and yelling. Explain that teachers have to talk to many children at once, and that people addressing any kind of group usually talk louder than they would in a private conversation. Remind your daughter that teachers have to raise their voices at times in order to get the attention of students who aren't listening. Even if the teacher is loud because she's angry, it doesn't necessarily mean that she's angry with your child.

Also, let your child know that teachers are human. They get irritated, have bad days, don't feel well at times, have personal pressures at home, and are subject to all the normal stresses of everyday living. If a teacher gets cranky, it doesn't mean the child has to take it personally. Remind your youngster of times when she's been in a grumpy mood, and tell her that the same thing can happen to a teacher.

But what about the occasion when the teacher really does yell at her students? If you suspect that this is the case, go to the counselor or principal and express your concern. Rather than accusing the teacher of improper behavior, raise the issue as a question. For example, you might say, "Mr. Thompson, Tammy has complained to me on several occasions that Mrs. Jones yells at the class. Are any of the other children in her class complaining about this?"

Even if the counselor or principal seems to stick up for the teacher, you can be certain that the matter will be looked into if several parents or children have complained about the same problem. The counselor or principal can also find an appropriate time to mention to the teacher that Tammy *thinks* that teacher is yelling. Most teachers will make an effort to talk to a child about this, providing an opportunity to reassure the youngster that the teacher is not angry with her. Also, it's good for teachers to be aware of the perceptions of their students, allowing them to monitor and change their own behavior, if necessary.

But what if, in spite of all your efforts to change things, the teacher continues to yell? You'll need to tell your child plainly that her teacher is just a yeller, and remind her not to take it personally. So long as the teacher's *words* are not emotionally abusive, you might need to teach your child that part of life involves adapting to people who do things that one might not like.

WHERE ARE THE HUGS?

Last year, Brent had a very warm, affectionate teacher whom he loved. This year, he doesn't seem happy about school, and you suspect it's because his new teacher has a more distant personality.

Like all of us, teachers have different personalities. While most parents of younger school children would probably pick a "touchy-feely" teacher for their youngster, if they had their choice, the fact is that many excellent teachers just aren't that physically affectionate with their students.

If your son has a rather matter-of-fact teacher who doesn't give lots of hugs and pats, or who doesn't use endearing words with her students, tell him that her lack of physical demonstrativeness doesn't mean that she's not a kind person, or that she doesn't like him. If he's just come from kindergarten and is used to sitting on a teacher's lap, let him know that elementary school is more "grown-up," and that children rarely sit on a teacher's lap there. Reassure him, of course, that he can still sit on your lap, and that you are up for lots of hugs!

It's important to realize that many teachers who are not very affectionate in class are still very positive with their students. They use praise liberally, and basically give out messages that a child is okay even when he makes a mistake. But what if a teacher is not only unaffectionate, but also comes across as negative and critical? This is the kind of teacher who notices what's *wrong*, but rarely remarks about what's *right*. Such a teacher can have a very negative impact on a student's self-esteem, as well as his feelings about school in general.

Talking to the Teacher

Whether or not the teacher is really critical, or your child just *perceives* her that way, the best first step is to talk to the teacher about the problem. Let her know that your child has commented that he feels he can never please her, and ask her if she has any idea why he would say this. Suggest that perhaps he doesn't notice the things she *does* praise him for, and ask her what these things are so that you can relay them back to him. If the teacher *is* giving him praise, she'll have several examples; if she *hasn't* been noticing the positive things about him, this is a gentle way to get her to begin noticing them.

You may find out, of course, that your child is not giving you the whole story. Perhaps he's not told you about times when he's behaved inappropriately. You might come away from your talk with the teacher with a very different view of the problem.

If you think your child is being overly sensitive to the teacher's making suggestions to him, let the teacher know about it. Perhaps there's something else going on in his life that's bothering him (not making friends, or a family problem) and he's not feeling too good about himself as a result. When a teacher understands what's going on emotionally with your child, she's in a better position to understand his reactions.

By pointing out to a teacher that your child is seeing her as negative and critical, she will probably make a genuine effort to be more positive with your youngster. Teachers want feedback from a parent if a child is upset with them, whether or not the youngster's perceptions are accurate. Most will use the feedback to monitor their own effectiveness, and to make changes when necessary.

But what if you come away from your talk with the teacher feeling that she really *is* critical and negative toward your child? Give her a little time to see what effect your talk with her has had. If nothing changes, it's time to discuss the situation with the counselor or principal.

A "PET" IN THE CLASS?

Amanda walks in the door from school and throws her backpack down in apparent disgust. When you ask her what's wrong, she tells you that her teacher is unfair and always favors Margie, whom everyone calls the "teacher's pet."

There are two possibilities to consider. The first is that Margie really is given preferential treatment by the teacher; the second is that Amanda is reacting to not getting something she wanted by blaming the teacher and Margie. How are you to know what's true?

Ask your daughter to tell you what actually happened that's upsetting her. Also ask for other examples of times when she thinks that the teacher favored Margie.

Then, ask her if there could be any *other* reason, besides

favoritism, that would cause the teacher *not* to select your child. For example, is your youngster not taking responsibility for something she is doing, or not doing, that could cause the teacher not to select her for something special? Perhaps Margie has earned her reward with exemplary behavior, and your child's complaint represents a sour-grapes attitude.

After this discussion, if you are reasonably convinced that the teacher actually *is* giving another child preferential treatment, tell your daughter that you think the matter should be brought up with the teacher. Since this would probably be a difficult subject for your child to initiate with a teacher, plan to do it yourself.

Explain to the teacher that your child thinks that the teacher doesn't like her as well as other children, relating some examples that your youngster has given. As with any talk with a teacher, state your concern in such a manner that you aren't seen as attacking the teacher, but simply trying to understand your child's perception of the situation.

If the teacher has been inadvertently favoring another child, your talk with her will certainly cause her to take a second look at her own behavior. Even more important, she'll be aware that your child is feeling left out in some way, and she can work on correcting the situation.

THE TEACHER WON'T EXPLAIN

Saul sits down to do his homework, but quickly gives up. He says that he can't do the work, insisting that the teacher didn't explain what he was supposed to do. When you ask him if he'd asked her for an explanation, he says, "No, because she won't answer my questions."

First, consider that Saul's perception that the teacher won't explain well could stem from a problem *he* is having. He might not listen attentively, or he might miss explanations and then repeatedly question her about things she's patiently explained several times. She might well refuse to answer his question if she sees that

Saul has been inattentive during her explanation, or if she's already addressed his question and thinks he's deliberately not paying attention.

This is a good example of a time when it can be tremendously helpful to have your child present when you confer with the teacher. Let her know that your son thinks she won't answer his questions, and then sit back and listen. Typically, the teacher will ask your child for examples of her ignoring him, or she might remind him of times when she would not answer him because of his prior behavior. As the two of them talk, it might become clear that your child is inattentive, oppositional, or simply trying to find a feeble excuse for not doing his schoolwork.

What is likely to be more difficult is to determine the reason behind your child's behavior. Does the problem occur throughout the day, or only when the teacher is discussing a certain subject? If he is inattentive only during math, perhaps he's having problems understanding math and hasn't wanted to admit it. If he's inattentive in the late morning, it may be that he's hungry and needs a bigger breakfast.

On the other hand, if a youngster is inattentive throughout the day, possible explanations might be that he's bored with the class material, that he's having vision or hearing problems, that he's being distracted by a child who sits near him, that he's preoccupied with something that's troubling him, that he's experiencing genuine learning difficulties, or that he has attention problems that keep him from being able to focus on a task. To get a clear picture of what is going on, it may be necessary for him to be evaluated by a psychologist. (For more information about psychological evaluation, see Chapter 9.)

Many times, the conference will reveal information that suggests a possible solution. The teacher and your child might agree on a plan to try to solve the problem (such as moving him to another seat in the classroom, or writing up a "contract" where he can earn some privilege for improved attention). If he blurts out something he's worrying about related to his family, peers, or himself, you can begin working with him on the problem.

It's also wise to ask the teacher to restate her rules about asking questions, if she doesn't bring it up. Perhaps your child speaks out when he has a question, and she requires the children to raise their hands. Maybe she asks her students to allow her to finish an explanation *before* she will accept questions. Does she allow a child to ask questions about material he doesn't understand during lunch, recess, before class, or after class? Many teachers arrange a special time of day when they want students to approach them about material that is not clear. The point is, make sure your child understands the procedure he needs to use when he's having trouble understanding the teacher.

Another possibility, of course, is *not* that the teacher won't answer questions, but that your child finds it hard to ask questions in class, and is projecting blame on the teacher to keep from admitting his problem. Many youngsters fear that they will be perceived as stupid if they ask a question, preferring to "fake it" rather than admit that they don't understand something.

Let your youngster know that asking questions is smart, not stupid. When someone asks a question, it shows that the person is thinking about what is being taught and is trying hard to understand it. Questions also help a teacher know what may be unclear about her explanation. Point out that when your child asks a question, there are likely to be other children who have the very same question. Just because his peers are quiet doesn't mean that everyone in the class understands everything perfectly.

WHEN YOUR CHILD IS KEPT IN AT RECESS

Barry has a tough time with written work, needing more time to complete it than most youngsters. He complains that he never gets time to play with his classmates because the teacher keeps him in during recess to finish his schoolwork.

Keeping a child from participating in recess is sometimes an appropriate consequence for a child who misbehaves in school. However, some youngsters find the *act* of writing to be laborious; it simply takes them longer to write legibly than some of their peers. These children have slow perceptual functioning for fine motor skills, such as writing, and are not just being obstinate. (For discussion of learning differences, see Chapter 9.) This type of child will typically need more time than his classmates to complete a written assignment. Taking away his recess privilege would have to be a daily event, which seems unfair punishment for a youngster who has writing problems. After all, recess provides a break from academics and also allows youngsters to socialize and to burn off pent-up energy.

Explain to your child that you understand it is really hard for him to complete his work as quickly as most of his classmates. He needs help, not punishment, so let him know that you will speak with the teacher about this issue.

When you talk with the teacher, tell her about your child's writing difficulty, if she's not already aware of it (she might think he's just being balky or careless). Let her know that you are not trying to get your child out of doing the classwork, but that you'd like to find a way for him to complete it without missing recess. Ask her to send unfinished classwork home for your child to finish in the evening. Most teachers are happy to do this, as long as they know you'll see to it that the child completes the work.

However, some children with this problem will end up having too much work in the evening. Once the teacher understands that the child is having to spend too much time doing homework at night, ask her if she might be willing to shorten his assignments to fit his level of capability.

Of course, there are some children who will prefer to stay in for recess to finish classwork rather than to take assignments home in the evening. If your son has friends, socializes well, and does not seem to need recess time for physical play, you might want to let him choose this option (so long as it's okay with the teacher). But if he tends to isolate himself from his peers, is overly dependent on being near the teacher, or is a very physical child who has difficulty sitting in class, it's best that he participate in recess and work out another solution for getting his assignments completed.

When your child has problems with handwriting, let him know that cursive writing (script) is usually easier than printing. Also, teach him to use a computer keyboard, word processor, or typewriter as soon as you can. Many communities have classes available to teach elementary-school children to type, and software is also available for children to learn typing on their home computers. It's not that he still won't have to write by hand in class; but his homework and book reports can be done much more easily once he learns to use a keyboard.

IS YOUR CHILD BORED?

Janie's teacher calls you for a conference and tells you that Janie doesn't listen in class. She thinks Janie might be having some type of emotional or academic problem, but you think that your daughter is simply bored.

You might be correct, but so could the teacher. Be glad the teacher brought the issue to your attention, and then begin some mutual problem-solving.

If Janie has problems listening early in her school career, it may be quite difficult to sort out the reasons for the problem. When a first-grader doesn't pay attention in class, the culprit could be an undetected learning difficulty and/or attention problem, an emotional issue, a hearing impairment, or boredom. Most teachers will try moving a child to another spot in the room, perhaps away from a bothersome neighbor, or to a spot right near the teacher's desk, to see if this helps. If not, they'll talk to a parent to see if the youngster might be reacting to something at home (birth of a baby, illness of a family member, marital conflict, etc.).

If a child also has problems listening at home, you would obviously want to rule out the presence of a hearing problem. Notice how the child responds to sounds from behind and to the side of her when she does not know you are there, and have her hearing checked if there's any question about her hearing acuity.

If the situation doesn't improve, educational and/or psychological testing is highly recommended. Even if a parent is correct about a child's being bored due to lack of challenge, testing is the best way to prove this hypothesis. Evaluation might reveal that the child has an underlying learning problem grasping the skills for reading, spelling, language processing, math, or written expression.

Testing might also help validate a teacher's impression that a child has attention difficulties, possibly including hyperactivity.

Such evaluation usually involves having both the teacher and a parent fill out one or more rating instruments that help separate issues of activity level, attention, distractibility, and oppositionalism. (For more information on testing and on hyperactivity, see Chapter 9.)

Emotional Causes

If Janie has been able to listen well in school before, then suddenly begins to have a problem paying attention, it makes sense to first consider the possibility that something is troubling her either about school or about her home life. You might have a hunch what the problem could be, or you might be totally baffled.

Either way, explain to Janie that if a person has trouble concentrating when normally she is able to focus her attention, the cause can be something that is bothering her. Ask her directly if she's worried about something. If she comes up with nothing, do some brainstorming of your own and check out your hunches with her. Examples might be saying something like "Do you think maybe you're missing Grandad since he died?" "Are you upset about not winning the election for class president?" "Are you still worried about that big fight your daddy and I had a couple weeks ago?" Explore your daughter's feelings about any issue that comes up. Even if you have no solution, know that your acknowledgment of her feelings and validation that those feelings are normal might be all that she needs to feel better. If your efforts to help her don't lead to improvement, you might consider having a consultation with a mental health professional to evaluate the situation in greater depth.

Boredom or Depression?

If you can't find a reason for your child's being upset, explore the boredom hypothesis. If she says that *is* the problem, most teachers are quite willing to find more challenging work for a child to do *after the youngster completes the regular assignment.* But the child needs to understand that she can't skip the work she's asked to do and just select what's personally interesting to her.

If you do determine that your child's problem is boredom and the teacher allows her to take on new challenges that are interesting to her *after* she finishes the required work, the child's listening problem should disappear. Such a child is also likely to need added intellectual stimulation out of school, so ask the counselor for information about learning-enrichment programs in your community.

The other factor to consider when your child complains of boredom is the possibility that she may be depressed. Is she also complaining of being bored at home? Does she pursue activities that she enjoys, or does she seem apathetic about most everything? Does she smile and laugh frequently, or does she seem serious or detached? If you suspect that she is depressed, consult a mental health professional.

SOMEONE'S CHEATING!

Elizabeth comes home upset because Erin got an A on a test by cheating while Elizabeth got an honest B. Elizabeth doesn't want to be a tattletale, but she's upset about the unfairness, and about the teacher's not knowing what's really going on.

Let Elizabeth know that you're proud of her for not approving of cheating, and sympathize with her about the unfairness in the situation with Erin. What you suggest next will depend on whether Erin cheated from *Elizabeth's* paper or from another child's paper.

If Erin copied Elizabeth's work, let your daughter know that her silence about the matter makes her an accomplice to the cheating. Suggest that she try to solve the problem with Erin first, letting Erin know that she doesn't want her work copied. She can remind Erin that there is a penalty for cheating when a person is caught, and that she doesn't want either of them to get in trouble. She might also offer to help Erin with work that Erin doesn't understand. However, Elizabeth needs to make it clear to Erin that she will have to tell the teacher if Erin continues to cheat from her paper.

However, if Erin is not directly involving Elizabeth in the

cheating, suggest that your child do nothing, since it really isn't any of *her* business. While cheating is dishonest, it isn't a crime and it isn't dangerous; she should only take it upon herself to interfere in someone else's private decision in the case of criminal activity or potential physical harm.

Explain to Elizabeth that if Erin continues to cheat, she will probably get caught by the teacher. Remind your daughter that, even if a cheater isn't caught in a particular instance, the cheater still loses. Not only does a cheater not learn the material she was supposed to learn, but she also must live with the guilty conscience of knowing that she has done something deceitful.

TOO MUCH HOMEWORK?

Your second-grader, Kirk, comes home from school most every day with homework that takes him over an hour to finish. It's not that he dawdles; it's just that the assignments require that much time. You want him to have some playtime and family time, but he doesn't have much of either.

Rather than approaching Kirk's teacher with your opinion that she's giving too much homework, talk to her about the length of time it takes your son to complete his assignments. Prepare in advance by jotting down examples of several specific evenings' homework and how long it took for Kirk to finish each part of it. She might be genuinely surprised by this information.

Of course, she might tell you that Kirk is making his homework more complicated than it need be. For instance, Kirk may be writing complete sentences when she only requires that he list one- or two-word answers.

If your child is taking a long time to finish homework and is not dawdling, chances are other children in the class are having the same problem. If the teacher tells you that she thinks the homework shouldn't take so long, and that Kirk must be stalling or is distracted, ask her if she's checked with some of the parents of Kirk's classmates to see how much time others are spending. If she discovers that most of the children have to spend too much time on homework, she's likely to change her assignments.

If you learn that other youngsters are finishing the same amount of work more quickly than your child is, that is valuable information. Unless there's a very obvious explanation (he's doing more work than is required for some reason, or he's not understanding necessary shortcuts), he'll need an educational evaluation to see if he has an underlying learning difficulty that has not been detected.

But what if you think that your child continues to have too much homework? Let the school counselor or principal know your concern, and she will look into the matter.

(For more information about homework problems, see Chapter 7.)

CHILD THINKS THE TEACHER DOESN'T LIKE HER

Shannon is upset. She tearfully tells you that her teacher doesn't like her.

Before you can give Shannon any advice, you'll want to know why she has arrived at her conclusion. Rather than jumping in to tell her that you're sure she's mistaken, first let her tell you her reasons for feeling the way she does.

The most common reason for a child to assume that a teacher dislikes her is that the teacher has criticized the child's behavior. It may be that she was told to talk more quietly in the lunchroom, to raise her hand before giving the answer to a question, to stay in her seat until the bell rings, to move to the back of a line, or any of a number of things teachers tell their students in the course of a day. Or perhaps the teacher wrote a critical comment on a returned paper.

Your child might feel even more upset if she perceives that the teacher acted unfairly. Perhaps other students were behaving the same way as your child, but your child is the one who got admonished for it. Or maybe your youngster made an innocent mistake and the teacher thought that it was deliberate. Perhaps the teacher accused your child of doing something she didn't do, or thinks she didn't do, such as starting a fight with a classmate.

If you think your youngster is being overly sensitive, let her know that a teacher's correction is part of the learning process. When teachers make these kinds of remarks to a student, or write corrections on a paper, it doesn't mean that the teacher doesn't like the child.

Perhaps your child is a perfectionist, and is upset because she made a mistake. Explain that everyone makes mistakes, and that a mistake serves a wonderful purpose: It allows a person to learn from a situation and, hopefully, to correct it. The point is not whether a person makes a mistake, but that the person learns from it.

If unfairness seems to be an issue, let your child know that teachers can't always see everything that's going on in a classroom. Just because other students are doing something they're not supposed to do doesn't justify your child's doing it. She still needs to pay the price if she's the one who's caught. To give her an example most children can relate to, point out that many drivers exceed the speed limit. Yet a driver who gets caught speeding still gets a ticket, even though he tells the policeman that many other drivers were speeding as well!

Perhaps your child feels she's been treated unfairly because she's been judged by her reputation. For example, if she's frequently caught whispering and giggling with other classmates while the teacher is speaking, she might be accused of such behavior at a time when she wasn't doing it. If that is the case, explain to your child that teachers make mistakes just like other people. It's not uncommon for adults, as well as children, to suspect a person who already has a reputation for misbehaving even when that person isn't guilty. Reassure her that changing a negative reputation takes time, and that she'll have to be patient before the teacher is likely to realize that the behavior has actually been changed.

If your daughter continues to feel that a teacher doesn't like her, bring up the matter with her teacher. Many times a teacher will shed further light on why your child might be feeling this way, and will also talk with your child to reassure her that *she* is liked even if some of her behavior is not. Remember, teachers want their students to feel liked by them, and will usually make an extra effort to reach out to a youngster who is feeling rejected.

YOU DISAGREE WITH TEACHER'S PERCEPTION

Sean's teacher has called you in for a conference and tells you that Sean is very uncooperative. You think your son has some type of learning problem, and that his seemingly uncooperative behavior is really his way of saving face when the work is too difficult for him.

Tell the teacher *why* you think your son is having a learning problem. Describe the strengths and weaknesses you've observed in working with him at home, pointing out any problem you've noticed in spelling, reading, math, writing, or following instructions. The teacher might follow through by doing a little individual work with your child to see if she notices the same kinds of problems you've noticed.

If the teacher remains unconvinced and continues to see your child as being uncooperative, the only informed way to settle the dispute is to have your child receive a psychological/educational evaluation. If the school is not able or willing to do such testing, find a public child guidance clinic, or a professional in private practice, who does this type of evaluation. (For more about these evaluations, see Chapter 9.)

Realize that many children who do have learning differences have emotional or behavior problems *as well*. In fact, the longer the learning difficulty goes undetected, the more likely it is that the child will develop maladaptive behavior. Rebellion, anxiety, or apathy are common emotional overlays for underlying learning problems.

Whether there is a learning difficulty or not, the child's uncooperative behavior still must be addressed through behavioral and motivational approaches (see Chapter 4 for more information). The learning problem should not become an excuse for misbehavior. At the same time, a child whose underlying learning difference is not discovered and addressed will continue to suffer frustration in academics. Having no explanation for his learning difference and no help in eliminating or compensating for it, he's likely to incorrectly think of himself as incapable or "stupid." The resulting damage to his self-esteem is obvious.

Most teachers are willing to try to accommodate the special needs of a child with a learning difference once the problem is correctly diagnosed. Schools also have special programs to help youngsters with such problems (discussed in Chapter 9).

Of course, it just might be that the teacher is correct, and the child's uncooperative behavior does not mask a learning difficulty. But the only way to accurately rule this out is to have the child evaluated through appropriate testing. (For suggestions about dealing with an uncooperative child who *doesn't* have a learning problem, see Chapter 5.)

IS THE GRADE UNFAIR?

Misty is very upset about the grade she received on her social studies test. She says several questions on the test were unclear, and that her answers were correct according to her interpretation. Unfortunately, her teacher thought differently and marked them wrong!

Unless you look at the test and see that Misty has overlooked something that would prove her wrong, suggest that she discuss her viewpoint with her teacher. If a child is hesitant about doing so, help her out by suggesting that she say something like "Mrs. Smith, I have a question about my test grade. When would be a good time to talk about it?" Encourage her to tell the teacher directly, but politely, that she thinks her answers to specific questions should be counted as correct, and then proceed to give her explanation.

Whether it's a test score, a grade on a homework paper, or a grade on a report card that your child thinks is inaccurate or unfair, advising her to discuss her feelings with the teacher encourages her to develop a healthy assertiveness. If she successfully makes her point and the teacher changes her mind, she'll feel an increased sense of competence.

What if the teacher refuses to change her mind, but you agree with your child's perception that the grade is unfair? Let your youngster know that you sympathize with her position and that you are proud of her for expressing her views to the teacher. Then remind her that the world is not always fair and that she doesn't need to make this molehill into a mountain by continuing to be upset. After all, a grade is only a grade, not a matter of life and death. Just knowing that *you* support her position, and that you are not going to make a big issue over her getting a lower grade than she might have deserved, will help her put the situation in perspective.

Of course, if several instances occur when you think a teacher is grading your child unfairly, you'd want to take up the matter directly with the teacher. Since almost nobody is thrilled to have mistakes called to their attention, it's best to help the teacher save face while you confront her on her errors. You might approach her by saying something like "I'm really confused about Misty's grade; if I understand your grading system correctly, I come out with a higher average" or, "I know you have so many papers to grade that it's impossible to get 100 percent accuracy, but I wanted to point out a few instances where I think a mistake was made on Misty's papers." The teacher will probably be most grateful for your tactfulness.

CHILD MISJUDGES HIS OWN LEVEL OF EFFORT

When you pick up Parker from school, you can tell by the look on his face that something upsetting has happened. He tells you that his teacher had a chat with him and told him that he wasn't working up to his potential. He thinks that he is working hard and that the teacher is wrong.

Ask Parker to tell you the details of the conversation with his teacher. What specific examples did she give him about *why* she thinks he's not working up to his potential? Did she say that he is wasting time in class, that he's not completing his work, that he does only the minimum that's required on his assignments, that he doesn't participate in class discussions, or give some other legitimate reason for her viewpoint?

If the teacher did have some good reasons for her opinion, help your son understand what he needs to change, and how to go about it. If you aren't clear about what is needed, talk to the teacher yourself, and then give your child feedback about your discussion, or include your child in the conference with you and the teacher.

Also be sure to ask your child to tell you specific examples of his working hard, and praise him for any that are accurate. Of course, it may be that he simply has a misconception about what is required to do well in school. For example, he might think that working on homework an average of fifteen minutes a night should be enough, when in reality, an hour of study would be more appropriate for his grade level. The point is to help your son get a clear sense of what is expected of him regarding school, both in class and at home.

But what if your child really *is* working conscientiously at his schoolwork? Perhaps the teacher has an unrealistic expectation about your child's level of capability, or an incorrect perception about the amount of effort he is putting into schoolwork. If this is the case, arrange to talk with the teacher and let her know about your son's study habits at home. Ask her for suggestions about how you can help him study more constructively, or about how you can work with him to help make his schoolwork easier.

WHEN YOU WANT A DIFFERENT TEACHER

Alice is just not doing well in school this year and dislikes her teacher. While you've talked with the teacher several times, you feel strongly that the teacher's personality is a negative factor for Alice. You've decided to ask the school to place Alice in a different class.

Before you request that the school place your daughter with a different teacher, you have to weigh several factors. First, if you are successful in getting the change, you are risking giving your child the message that you'll step in and be able to fix whatever is not going her way. In reality, you can't fix everything for her (nor should you, even if you could). Just because a youngster doesn't like a particular teacher is not enough reason to justify switching her to another one, *except in the case when you think your child's emotional well-being will be jeopardized.* Obviously, this is a highly individual matter, but might occur if your daughter becomes depressed or very anxious due to her classroom situation.

Second, you have to consider the available teacher options. Whether there's only one or several other teachers for your child's grade, you want to be sure that the new teacher will be an improvement. That will mean doing some research. The school counselor would be a good resource, as she should be most familiar with the teaching styles, quirks, and personalities of all the teachers on staff. She is also likely to know whether or not there are some children in the new class who might create even more problems for your child. If you know some parents of students who have the teacher you're thinking of requesting, talk with them as well.

Third, schools do not like to change a child's teacher except in rare circumstances. Such action can encourage other parents to request changes, especially if your child's teacher is not very popular with her other students and/or their parents.

Fourth, parents who ask for a teacher change are sometimes viewed negatively by school personnel. If you request this special consideration for your child, you may risk *not* getting special consideration at a later time. You'll want to make sure that you use this power judiciously.

After weighing all of these factors, you might still decide that you are going to ask for a teacher change. When you discuss this with the principal, focus on specific behaviors relating to your child and the teacher, rather than making an emotional plea. If you have more than one option for a new teacher, tell the principal what type of teacher you think will be best for your child (more structured, more affectionate, etc.), and why you have made such a determination. Unless you have a specific reason for asking for one teacher over several, it's better to let the principal select. Many parents automatically ask for the most popular teacher when another choice would better suit their child's needs.

Probably some of the hardest feelings between parents and school personnel occur when a parent's request to change teachers is denied. If this happens to you, listen carefully to the reasons you are given for the refusal. Although it is difficult to remain objective in this circumstance, the school might have a valid point. Obviously, if you still disagree, you'll probably have to place your child in a different school if you don't want to acquiesce to the school's decision. Of course, you'll want to consider how much of the school year is left. Your child might be better off waiting out the year rather than going through a transition to a new school, new teacher, and new classmates. If you're considering switching your child to a private or parochial school, realize that many will not accept a new student late in a school year.

CHAPTER 4

When Your Child Is Having Social Problems

YOUR CHILD WILL LEARN MUCH MORE THAN JUST THE "THREE R's" in school. It is the social context that will teach him how to get along with other people, especially his peers. Whether he feels good or bad about himself will be greatly influenced by how his classmates view him.

As a parent, you can feel especially stymied when your child has social problems at school. After all, you're not around to see the action. It's not as simple as monitoring children playing in your own backyard. There, you can see directly what your child has to deal with and what his friends are really like. Even better, you can see exactly how your child might contribute to his own problem. You can also step in and take control of the situation if it should become necessary.

But what happens when your son comes home from school crying because he's been rejected by his classmates? Or if the teacher calls to tell you that he is being bullied on the playground? Your protective instincts might immediately rise as you think, "Why are those mean kids picking on my child?" At the same time, the more objective side of you might wonder if your son is responsible, at least in part, for the problem he's having. If the same complaint has occurred before, you're likely to feel even more frightened, frustrated, angry, hurt, sad, confused, and/or helpless.

Even if you know why your child is having a particular social problem with other children, kids typically see any problem as the "other guy's" fault. Getting a child to admit to his own responsibility in creating the problem is not easy. If you persist in trying to convince him that he's reacting inappropriately, no matter how logical your argument, he's unlikely to be swayed. Even worse, he might feel totally unsupported as he becomes convinced that you don't understand and/or believe him.

Since the direct "here's what you're doing wrong and how to correct it" approach will rarely be effective, you'll probably need to find more indirect ways to help your child with social problems. This might involve your telling stories about children or animals that exemplify the point you're trying to get across, doing some creative role playing with your son, and/or getting him involved in structured situations where he'll have a more positive peer experience (church activities, sports, etc.). Remember that you can also ask your child's teacher or counselor for ideas about how to help your son during the school day.

COMMON PROBLEM SITUATIONS

NO FRIENDS

Ellie races in from school to look at the mail, searching for a birthday party invitation from a classmate. When she sees none, she runs up the stairs to her room and slams the door exclaiming, "I knew it! I don't have any friends!"

Your response to Ellie will obviously be different if she *does* have friends than if she is, in fact, shunned or ignored by her schoolmates. If she's exaggerating and does have one or more friends at school, it's tempting to jump in and point this fact out to her. But hold back a little, and try to find out why this particular party invitation is so important to her. Perhaps the classmate who is having the party is a peer of high status, and Ellie feels she's not a part of the "popular" group of children. Maybe she has considered this other child to be a friend, heightening her disappointment in not receiving an invitation.

Reflect your daughter's distress with a sympathetic comment like "I know you're really disappointed, honey." Then you might inquire, "What's so special about this particular party, anyway?" Hearing your daughter's reasons for feeling upset gives her a chance to feel understood, and gives you the opportunity to gain insight into what's really bothering her.

Once she's had a chance to ventilate her feelings, your statement about her having other friends is more likely to register. Remind her that some parties are small, so only a few kids can be invited.

This can also be a good time to let her know that, even if the girl giving the party doesn't like her, *everyone* runs into people who don't particularly like them. In other words, nobody can expect to be liked by everyone they meet. This doesn't mean that either person is wrong or bad, but simply that they don't feel drawn to one another for some reason.

At this point, your child might come up with a possible reason that the other youngster doesn't like her; for example, she might tell you that the other child is jealous of her for making better grades, for having more boys in the class talk to her, or for receiving some class honor.

If you think that your daughter is correct in her assessment that she doesn't have friends in school, have a talk with her about how a person makes friends. Ask her to name a child in her class who is well liked, and then ask her to tell you *why* she thinks that child is so popular: "What does Jenny do that makes all the kids like her so much?"

Strategies That Work

It is also helpful to give your child some strategies for making friends. The main point to get across is that she needs to act *friendly*. This means talking with people, smiling at them when appropriate, and being willing to share toys, activities, or property. Many children don't realize how important it is to be *actively* friendly.

If you have some hunches about why your child is experiencing problems with her peers, it's best to help her discover the reasons herself, rather than to tell them to her directly. You can accomplish this nicely by saying something like "Well, honey, why don't you tell me some things kids do that other kids don't like? Then you can decide if you do any of those things." It might help to take out a sheet of paper and begin listing the behaviors your daughter mentions, adding ideas of your own when she gets stuck. By the time the two of you finish this exercise, you might have a list that looks something like this:

> bosses people around
> cries when she doesn't get her way
> teases too much
> puts other people down
> pushes people around
> won't take turns
> always has to win or be first
> won't follow rules
> hits
> argues
> tattles
> lies
> acts snobby
> gossips
> butters up the teacher
> interrupts other people
> uses foul language
> acts like a know-it-all

Once the list is complete, ask your child if she ever does any of the things on the list. Chances are she'll admit to one or two, giving you the opportunity to congratulate her for figuring out what she's doing that could be alienating her classmates. If she denies doing anything on the list, gently point out the items you've noticed in her behavior, or that you've heard about from a reliable source, giving her specific examples if possible.

You might also enlist a teacher or counselor's help when your child has trouble making friends. Many times, school personnel can come up with creative ways to include a child in some project or activity with another classmate or two who would be likely candidates for friendship with your child, or who could positively influence your child's behavior. Also, alerting a teacher about the problem can help her be more sensitive to kids ganging up on your child.

Certainly, you don't want to forget the tried-and-true ways that you can help your child develop friendships. This would include making it a point to have her invite one or two friends over after school or on the weekend, or even letting her host a party of her own. If she continues to have difficulty making friends at school, get her involved in clubs, sports, lessons, church, or other group activities where she has the opportunity to develop friendships with a different group of youngsters.

OVERLY CONCERNED ABOUT POPULARITY

Frank is very easily influenced by his peers and is getting into trouble as a result. Fearing that he won't be well liked, he can't say "No" to anything his classmates suggest. You're worried that he'll do anything to be popular.

Let Frank know that kids who are overly concerned about being popular depend constantly on the approval of their peers. They always feel the pressure to be "on," which can be exhausting, since opinions about who's popular and who's not can change overnight. By always trying to please their peers, such children don't have a chance to develop a firm sense of who *they* really are.

Also, some children seem popular simply because they can be talked into doing anything. Consequently, their peers often dare them to do things that can get the naive youngster into trouble. The truth is that other kids make fun of those who can be so easily led (behind the victim's back, of course).

On the other hand, youngsters whose popularity *lasts* are those who are friendly, treat others fairly, and can be counted on to respect the rights of other people. Such a person stands up for what he believes in, even when others disagree. This kind of popularity makes a person a leader, unlike the popularity gained by a person who can be talked into anything out of fear of being rejected. The truly popular youngster is liked for who he is, *not* for what others expect or want him to be.

In addition to explaining the distinction between true and false popularity, you'll also want to think about *why* your child is so vulnerable to peer pressure. Typically, his quest to be popular stems from some underlying insecurity he's trying to cover. He might worry that he's not athletic, that he's stupid, that he's too big, that he's not attractive, or any of a number of things that can cause his peers to reject him. By figuring out what's really bothering him and then addressing that problem, you'll bolster his sagging self-esteem. The higher his self-esteem, the less vulnerable he will be to the expectations of his peers in a quest for false popularity.

But what if your child feels insecure about something neither you nor he can really solve at the moment? Perhaps he has to endure crooked teeth, a learning difference, being the shortest person in his class, and so on. It will be important to find other strengths and talents in your son that will help him to feel good about himself in spite of some negative characteristic. Also, don't insult him by denying the truth. You can sympathize with his problem or difference, letting him know that you know it's tough for him. Give him appropriate reassurance (that he will grow, that he can get his teeth fixed some day, that being unathletic won't seem so important when he's a grown-up, that you will get him appropriate help for his learning problem, etc.).

BUYING FRIENDSHIP

The teacher calls to tell you that Annette often gives the best part of her lunch, her money, or her personal belongings to her classmates. The teacher feels that Annette's behavior is not an act of generosity, but an attempt to buy friendship.

Just as the child who is overly concerned with popularity, the youngster who tries to buy friendship is insecure about her ability to make and keep friends. She picks the easy way to get seemingly instant friendship by giving presents to anyone she wants to like her.

Point out to your daughter that friends who are "bought" are usually fair-weather friends at best. Of course, they'll act as if they are good friends, but the bond usually stops when the giver runs out of goodies to give! Even more upsetting, peers are quick to make fun of the child who gives presents to gain friends.

Of course, it's unlikely that your child will admit that she is actually trying to buy friends. She'll probably insist that she's simply trying to "be nice." Accept her explanation about her motivations, but tell her that her actions are *perceived* by other children to be an attempt to buy friendship. Let her know that there are other ways to "be nice," such as being friendly, giving sincere compliments, and being a good listener. You might also suggest that she offer to trade items rather than simply giving her things away.

Talk with your daughter to find out why she might feel unable to make friends by just being herself. Address her underlying insecurity with information and/or reassurance, just as you would with the child who worries about popularity (see situation above).

SHYNESS

Juan has always been quiet and shy. The teacher says that he won't participate in class discussions, and that he doesn't socialize with his classmates.

It's important to determine whether or not a child is simply *shy,* which is a normal aspect of personality, or whether he's *withdrawn,* which can suggest a deeper emotional problem. Although the distinction can sometimes be difficult, the shy child usually will open up, given a little time to become familiar with a new situation. Once he begins to feel comfortable, he'll become increasingly more talkative and will participate normally in peer activities.

The child who is withdrawn usually will not increase his participation even after a sufficient time has passed for him to become comfortable in a new situation. He is less reachable emotionally, and even the best efforts to draw him out or to get him involved in a familiar activity will fail. Often, the child's withdrawal covers an underlying depression. Consultation with a mental health professional is definitely recommended if you feel your child is withdrawn.

You can help a shy child in several ways. First, reassure him that there is nothing wrong with him, that he simply needs a little more time to become comfortable in a new situation than a more outgoing child. If children tease him about being shy, he can say something like "I'm just quiet, but I'm listening" or "It just takes me a little time to warm up to people."

Point out to a shy child that he's likely to feel more comfortable socially if he's involved in some structured activity (a sport, a game, putting a puzzle together). When he meets a new friend, he can suggest something specific for the two of them to do to break the ice. He can then make conversation related to the activity rather than having to think up new topics.

Also, give him some simple conversation tips. Asking questions about another child's interests is always a good idea, and can be started with a simple "What do you like to do for fun?" or "What do you like to play?" Asking another child if he's seen a popular movie, television show, sports event, or video game is another good conversation starter, followed by, "What did you like best about it?"

Some younger children respond well to role playing with puppets. Play out situations that the child is likely to encounter in the classroom, on the playground, and in the neighborhood, demonstrating how to be friendly and how to show interest in the other party. With just a few well-rehearsed responses under his belt, the shy child can more easily get a converation going that will take off spontaneously on its own.

It can also help to involve a shy child in structured peer group activities, such as Scouts, a church group, or a sports team. By being involved in a number of peer groups, he has a chance to grow more comfortable being around kids his age.

LOSING A BEST FRIEND

Jill found out in school that her best friend, with whom she's grown up, has decided to be another girl's best friend. Although Jill announced this situation stoically and hurried to her room, you hear her crying behind her closed door.

Go to Jill's room and sit with her, put your arms around her (if she doesn't resist) and comfort her while she cries. Be with her, offering your quiet support, until she's ready to talk. Just being physically close to your daughter when she's emotionally upset can often be more comforting than any words you could say.

When she's calmer and ready to discuss the situation, ask her to tell you what happened. Listen to her story first before giving your own interpretation or advice. Let her know how very sorry you are that this has happened, and that you certainly understand why she's upset.

Many parents try to help a child feel better about such a situation by minimizing its importance, which only makes the youngster feel misunderstood. Losing a best friend *is* important. Being told that there are lots of other nice girls to be friends with, that you're sure the friend will change her mind, that she and her friend were always arguing anyway, or that she should be glad to discover that her friend wasn't such a good friend after all will not be at all comforting, even if true.

Give your child some explanation about why friends might decide to go their separate ways. After all, people change. As they grow up, children often develop new interests and, of course, will begin friendships with other youngsters who have those same interests. If this is the case, tell your child something like "Honey, Jan has really been excited about getting on the gymnastics team. It's only natural that she would begin to be closer with some of the other girls on the team since she spends so much time with them." Or, "I've noticed that you and Jan don't seem to have as much fun when you get together as you used to. Sounds like she's not so interested in playing with dolls anymore. Some girls at your age just change their interests."

Sometimes you or your child will think that the friend left for selfish reasons. For example, perhaps she wanted to be with a more popular child, or with one whose family treats their child's friends to special gifts or events. If this seems to be so, let your child know that true friends do not break up a friendship for such reasons, and that this makes a negative statement about the other child's character.

Also, let your daughter know that friendships can form and break up rapidly in the elementary-school years. Kids who aren't speaking one day will be chums the next. If this seems to be the case with your child's classmates, encourage your youngster to remain friendly with everyone and not to join in the negative gossip that goes on so often in such situations. Tell her that the kids who end up being well liked, especially as they get older, are those who don't take sides in other kids' disputes and who don't say unkind things about anyone.

Point out to your child that you know she'll miss her best friend, but that she will be able to make another. Once a person learns how to be a friend, she always keeps that ability. Suggest that she think of some of the girls she's friendly with and invite one or more of them to begin spending time with her. Let her know that it's perfectly okay not to have a "best friend" for a while, at least not until she finds someone who really feels right for that position.

But what if all your child's peers are already paired off in friendships, or there are cliques that will not include her? If this unfortunate situation occurs, let your child's teacher and/or counselor know about it. Sometimes they will find good ways to bring youngsters together in a project or an activity that allows for a friendship to develop. Try to find other sources of friendship for your child in your neighborhood: a church or synagogue youth group, or an organization such as Scouts.

ENTERING SCHOOL MIDYEAR

A job change has resulted in your moving to a new town. While you're pleased about your new location, you're a little worried about how Belinda, your fourth-grader, will be able to make friends in the middle of the school year.

No doubt, Belinda is also a little worried about whether or not she'll be able to make friends at the new school. Let her know that you understand her fears, and that they are normal. But remind her that once a person knows how to make one friend, she knows how to make many. It just takes being kind and acting friendly.

Let your daughter know that she'll make friends more quickly if she *actively* seeks them. In other words, encourage her to introduce herself and to ask questions: "What's fun to do around here?" "Where do you like to shop?" "Do they have meatloaf in the cafeteria every Wednesday?" "Does our teacher give lots of homework?" "What good shows are on TV tonight?"

If your child goes to a neighborhood school, encourage her to invite other kids who live nearby to visit your home. If she goes to a private or parochial school, let her know that you are willing to invite a classmate over either after school or on the weekend, so long as she checks with you first. You might even suggest that she have a small party to celebrate an upcoming holiday.

When you enroll your daughter in the new school, ask if they have a "buddy" system for new students. Many schools assign volunteer students to show a new child around the school, to sit with the newcomer at lunch, and to introduce her to a few students. If your child seems to be lonely those first few days in the new school, be sure to let the teacher know right away. Most teachers are good about helping a new child fit in by drawing them into conversations with other students, and even helping to pair them with youngsters who seem to be a good match.

THE UNATHLETIC BOY

Trevor has never been much of an athlete, and the kids in gym class embarrass him by making fun of his fumbling efforts. How can you help him cope with this unfortunate situation?

Kids can be very cruel to a peer who doesn't fit the stereotypical role for his or her sex. This affects boys who are unathletic and, to a somewhat lesser degree, girls who are "tomboys." If your child is ridiculed for not fitting a sex-role stereotype, you'll need to explain this information to him. Let him know that these stereotypes will become less important as he grows up, as most adults don't make such a big deal out of men or women who have nontraditional interests or talents.

This explanation, of course, is not going to eliminate the fact that it's no fun being ridiculed by one's peers. Point out to your child that all people have strengths and weaknesses, and let him know what you consider his strengths to be. Try to get him to handle the ridicule by taking a good-humored approach. For example, he might say, "Come on, guys, quit bugging me. You know I'm not cut out for this stuff!" or "Give me a break! Sports are just not my thing!" or even, "Okay! What lucky team is going to get me?" If your child can muster this kind of light retort, chances are the children who tease him will back down.

But what if your son is too shy or embarassed to stick up for himself? If you think his self-esteem is suffering, talk to the gym teacher about your concern. She might be willing to give your child a little extra individual instruction, such as tips on ball throwing. Or she might be able to assign your child a job, such as scorekeeper, timekeeper, or equipment manager, which would gracefully get him out of this difficult situation. In a case where a youngster continues to be ridiculed, you might ask the principal or counselor to remove him from class to do some school job (helping out in the attendance office, being a teacher's runner) during his gym period. Be aware that the school may need a written request from a physician or mental health professional to waive a physical education requirement.

Unfortunately, a child's early difficulty with a physical skill or a sport will often perpetuate itself unnecessarily. A boy gets a message that he lacks coordination or ability in early childhood, and then gives up because he fears further ridicule. However, some children who are not talented in the typical team sports that are played in elementary school (football, baseball, soccer) might learn to do quite well in a sport such as swimming, tennis, golf, gymnastics, or karate. Also, many kids prefer these more individualized sports to those that emphasize working with a large team. Even if a child never becomes a star in such activities, he can at least develop further coordination skills that he would never improve on otherwise. More important, he can gain confidence and enjoyment from some kind of physical activity.

It is also possible to enroll your child in a class that is specifically designed to improve coordination and motor skills. Ask your counselor, a local child-guidance clinic, a university education or physical education department, or an occupational therapist for information about these classes. It's not that such classes will turn your son into a natural athlete, but they can help him gain more confidence and skill about moving his body in space, perhaps giving him the boost he needs to go on and participate in some sports activity.

EMBARRASSED ABOUT PUBERTY

Laura is the only fourth-grade girl who needs a bra. You notice that she's started wearing a jacket even when she's not outside, and that she wants to buy only loose-fitting clothes that are a size too big.

A girl who enters puberty in fourth or fifth grade often has a difficult time accepting it. It's hard enough to get used to a new body, but it's even harder when she looks so different from everyone else her age. A girl who develops large breasts may be particularly susceptible to peer ridicule, as other girls tend to concoct wild stories (implying sexual activity) about why she is so well endowed, while the boys not-so-subtly ogle her.

If your daughter is an early maturer, talk with her about her feelings on the matter. Let her know that she's perfectly normal, even though she's developing earlier than most of her peers. Reassure her that in a year or two, she'll have lots of company.

In the meantime, be sensitive to her self-consciousness, and respect her wish to minimize her chest. Get her a well-fitting bra, and let her buy some attractive sweaters, vests, or sweatshirts (or, if it's warm, loose-fitting tops that can't be seen through) to replace the jacket.

THE VICTIM OF A BULLY

Tim suddenly states that he doesn't want to go to school anymore. As you explore his feelings, you find out that he's afraid of a larger boy who is bullying him.

While your first impulse might be to tell your son, "Just ignore the bully!" you should realize that this common advice rarely works. The only time that ignoring a bully *might* work is when the bully taunts a child for the first time. Getting no initial reaction, the bully is more likely to pick on another youngster who will give him the satisfaction he's seeking by becoming upset or angry. By the time a child is consistently being bullied, however, it's usually too late for this ignoring tactic to be effective.

Basically, a child who is being bullied needs to say something to the taunter to show that he's not frightened, but he must do so without provoking a fight or escalating a challenge. Comments like "Oh, grow up!" or "Come on, cut it out!" or "Yeah, right!" are good responses. The victim can then walk away, perhaps right past the bully, or join another group of youngsters nearby.

Explain to your child that bullies love to get their victims to cry, to look rattled, or to explode in angry shouting or a temper fit. Such a reaction lets the bully know he's gotten to the victim, and that the bully has won. When the victim gets into trouble with the teacher for an angry outburst, the bully reaps even greater satisfaction.

Try role playing with your child until he is able to give appropriate and convincing responses to a bully's taunting. By hearing himself practice in the safety of his home, he's likely to gain more confidence than if he just talks about how he *could* respond.

You might wonder if it is ever appropriate to tell your child to stand up to a bully by challenging him, even if such action could result in a physical fight. Obviously, if the bully is significantly bigger than your youngster, if he's carrying a weapon, or if your child is alone and is being threatened by a *group* of youngsters, let your child know that a direct challenge is simply not worth the risk of getting seriously hurt. However, if significant physical danger is not an issue, your child might actually enhance his self-esteem (and his peers' esteem of him!) by standing up to the bully and risking a physical fight. Even if he ends up with a bloody nose or a black eye, the bruise to his ego could be more damaging if he doesn't take the risk of standing up to the bully. Also, a bully is less likely to continue picking on a child who has been willing to stand up for himself.

Make sure that your child knows that you expect him to react to a bully by first trying nonconfrontational tactics, and that you don't want him to *initiate* a physical fight. However, if the bully persists in taunting him, it might be best to draw the line and risk a fight. In fact, many times a bully will back down when confronted.

THE BRUNT OF NAME-CALLING

Lately, Marianne has been coming home from school in tears. She complains that her classmates make fun of her and call her terrible names.

It can be difficult to help your child understand that the best way to react to name-calling or teasing of any type (even if the teasing is about *real* characteristics, such as having a big nose, being overweight, doing poorly in school) is *not to react*! Telling her the old adage that "Sticks and stones may break my bones, but names can never hurt me" is not enough. In fact, *telling* her anything will probably not be of much help. It's *practicing* the art of nonreaction that can make the difference.

A very effective way to extinguish your child's problematic

response to name-calling is to set up a game in which you, the child, and other family members (the more players, the better) sit in a circle and practice calling each other the same kinds of names that your child is being called. Let yourself, or another adult, be "It" and say something like "I bet you can't call me *any* name that can get me upset!" Then, have everyone else, including the child, shout ridiculous names at the person. The one who's "It," of course, shows that she's not at all rattled by any of the names, challenging the others by making remarks such as, "Come on, guys, you can do better than that!" or "Sorry, I'm just not upset!" Be sure to use not only the names the child has actually been called by her peers, but also names that make silly rhymes with "It's" name ("Judy the Cootie!" or "Mom the Bomb!"), or even nonsense syllables ("You gubber-blum!"). The more the players act like they're really trying to make "It" get upset, the more quickly everyone will begin laughing at how ridiculous the whole situation is.

Let the child who's been the victim of name-calling take her turn last. Be sure to repeat the names she's been called many times, as well as names that rhyme with hers ("Marianne the Frying Pan!"). By this time, she'll probably begin giggling as soon as the first silly name is spoken. When it's clear that she no longer reacts negatively to the name-calling, congratulate her for learning how not to react to such teasing. You might also plant the suggestion that, from that time on, she'll probably not be able to stop herself from having a little smile inside (perhaps even outwardly) when someone tries to upset her by calling her names.

Such a demonstration of the fact that names cannot hurt a person provides a wonderful lesson for your child. Even more important, it allows her to feel powerful because she has successfully changed her response to this kind of teasing. This teaches her your message much better than any words of advice you could give her.

DEALING WITH REJECTION

Jimmy has a noticeable speech problem that results in his being rejected by his classmates. Despite the teacher's best efforts to get the other children to be nice to him, Jimmy is well aware that he really doesn't have a true friend in his class.

Unfortunately, kids can be very unfair and hurtful to one another. Children who look, dress, or behave very differently are often targets of ridicule and rejection by their peers. Prejudice about a child's race, physical handicap, or family circumstances (poverty, parent in jail, etc.) can also contribute to a youngster's being scapegoated by classmates.

Whatever the reasons for a child's rejection by peers, it is heartbreaking for parents to see their children struggling against such unfairness. Responses like "Just don't pay any attention to those kids—you're better than they are, anyway!" or "Who cares what those kids think?" or "Why do you let yourself get so upset over something like that?" are not at all helpful.

What a rejected child needs is to have his hurt and angry feelings acknowledged by a parent, not denied or rationalized. Let him know that you do understand why he's upset, and that his reaction is normal. Reassure him that children are not mature enough to understand the total situation, but as they grow up, people usually become more tolerant and accepting. In all likelihood, he'll not experience the rejection he's receiving in childhood once he's an adult.

Be sure to give your child some explanation about why you think his peers are rejecting him. For example, if racial or social discrimination is involved, you would give him some history about such prejudice and tell him what is being done to change it. Let him know that discrimination in people stems from their fear and insecurity about anyone or anything that is "different."

For another example, consider the case of a child who is rejected because of illness, a handicap, or something unusual about his personal appearance. Explain that people who are not mature respond to such differences out of fear. Such problems remind them of their *own* vulnerability to sickness, accidents, and other things that are out of their control. However, the true measure of a person is not what his body looks like, but the qualities that are on the *inside* of a person. The point is that you want to help your child understand not only the surface reason that he's being rejected, but also the underlying dynamics for such treatment.

It's very helpful to tell your youngster a childhood experience of your own in which you were rejected, treated unfairly, or ridiculed. This kind of sharing strengthens your parental bond with your child, provides a healthy example to model, and gives him added emotional support.

Then, most important, look around your community for groups made up of other children who share your child's particular predicament, or for groups where your child will get a friendly reception. Develop his talents with appropriate lessons, classes, camps, and other activities that will build his self-esteem. Of course, you'll want to continue communicating with the teacher and counselor to enlist their help in finding ways to reduce the rejection your child experiences in school.

PEER PRESSURE ABOUT CLOTHES

Mandy goes to school in an especially affluent area of town. Most of her peers wear expensive clothes and accessories that you can't afford, and Mandy complains that her classmates make fun of her because of her wardrobe.

Of course, you'll want to explain to Mandy that people who judge others by their clothes are being very shallow. Unfortunately, kids are immature by nature, so they will often make such judgments. Although this explanation is true and needs to be said, it will not do much to help Mandy's predicament.

Because a child's self-esteem is so important, and because peer reaction contributes greatly to a child's perception about herself, you'll want to do whatever you *reasonably* can do to help your daughter fit in with the way her peers dress. This does not mean that you should take on an extra job or make some major sacrifice in order to buy your child more expensive clothes. But you can be sensitive to how your child's appearance could look *less* different from that of her peers.

For example, if the girls in your child's class all wear hair bows, you can buy or make some inexpensive hair bows. Accessories usually don't have to be "designer" items; just *having* that accessory is what counts. Many times a child will feel she's right in fashion by changing just one thing about her appearance. It could be wearing a watch, having lace on her socks, or having a necklace with a popular cartoon character on it that does the trick. Or it might be that you'd allow her to *stop* wearing something that her peers ridicule. Examples might be skirts that are the "wrong" length, the style of shoes (tennis shoes instead of loafers, or vice versa), hair in a barrette (the other girls wear ponytail holders), and so on.

You might also go through a magazine with your daughter, pointing out "looks" that are popular, and then help her go through her wardrobe to see what can be made more fashionable (changing the length of a skirt, adding new buttons to a shirt). Make a list of items that can go with many outfits (a vest, a belt, a shirt of a particular color) and then look for those items the next time you are ready to shop.

Another option is to allow your child to have some choice of an expensive item. For example, she might choose to have one pair of the popular, more expensive jeans, *or* the two pairs of inexpensive jeans you were originally planning to buy for her. Again, having just one "in" item can do wonders for her feeling of fitting in with her peer group.

You might be thinking, "Well, why give in to a materialistic, superficial value system? Why not just teach your child that such a viewpoint is wrong, and that you'll not support it?"

Realize that you, as an adult, have formed a strong belief that would support such action. However, your child does not yet have the maturity to have this conviction, and is far more concerned with being acceptable to her peers. If you bought all the expensive clothes she wanted and granted her every whim, you would be teaching her to be materialistic. But if you make an effort to help her fit in with her peers to a greater degree, without going overboard, you will teach her that you are sensitive to her feelings and that you are supportive of her. Most of all, you'll help reduce the peer ridicule she is suffering.

WHEN YOU NEED TO GET INVOLVED IN YOUR CHILD'S PROBLEM WITH ANOTHER CHILD

Ed is suddenly scared to walk home from school. He says that Brian, an older boy in his school, chases him, grabs his backpack, and strews the contents all over the sidewalk. While Ed hastily retrieves his belongings, Brian threatens that one day soon he's going to beat up "the wimp."

This situation represents much more than simple teasing or bullying. No adult supervision is available, and Brian's behavior is emotionally and physically intimidating, since he is older and bigger than Ed.

As a general rule, it's best to allow a child to work out a conflict with a peer without adult interference. He needs to learn how and when to stand up for himself, how to negotiate, and how to compromise. He also needs to feel an increasing sense of personal control over life's problems and challenges as he grows up. There are exceptions to this rule, however, especially if other possible solutions have not worked or are not available.

In Ed's case, a parent might first suggest that Ed walk home with a couple of his peers, or with an older child. It might also be possible for him to walk a different route and avoid the bully. However, these solutions might not work or might not be possible.

If Ed's problem occurred on school property, it would be appropriate to discuss the situation with school personnel. They might be able to handle the problem by confronting the bully and/ or by keeping a closer eye on both Ed and Brian. However, when a youngster is placed in a dangerous, illegal, and/or emotionally abusive situation, and there is no structured supervision, it's time for a parent to step in directly.

If you can find out where the offender lives, or his parents' name, you can call or visit the youngster's parents to discuss the matter. You'll be more likely to avoid a defensive reaction if you remain matter-of-fact and begin with a statement such as, "I think our boys are having a problem that we need to discuss." Then state the information you have, perhaps setting up a meeting between yourself, the other boy's parents, and the two youngsters.

Of course, if your child is being bullied on your own property and is in potential danger, or is obviously unable to stand up for himself, you would step in and take charge of the situation. If this happens, be sure to explain to your child afterward your reasons for your behavior. He might feel embarrassed at your actions, or that you've treated him like a "baby." Let him know how the incident differed from more normal circumstances when you would not interfere and would expect him to handle the situation on his own.

There is another time that you might want to intervene in your child's conflict with a peer even if danger, illegal action, or abuse are not involved. Sometimes a child is simply not emotionally capable of standing up for himself. While you would suggest ways in which he could do so, he just might not be up to it due to immaturity, excessive shyness, or prior trauma in his life. Rather than allow him to continue to suffer simply because he won't take action on his own, it would be appropriate to step in directly and become his advocate.

CHAPTER 5

When Your Child Gets into Trouble

WHEN YOU RECEIVE YOUR CHILD'S REPORT CARD, YOU PROBABLY look first at her grades. But the other half of the report card, the "conduct" side, also gives you a lot of important information. It is here that you'll find out about your youngster's work habits as well as her level of attention, independence, cooperation, and socialization.

It's obvious that a child's conduct problems can have a great impact on her grades. Students who are uncooperative, inattentive, bothersome to other classmates, rude, or argumentative are more likely not to do their best work. Teachers are only human, and if a child has a borderline grade at report-card time, they'll understandably decide on the lower mark for a student who has poor conduct.

The solution to a child's conduct problems depends greatly on good communication between parent and teacher, sometimes with the added help of the school counselor. A teacher needs to have your support in giving your child the message that *you* expect her to behave in school just as much as the teacher does. Sometimes it becomes necessary to demonstrate this support by directly tying a child's after-school privileges at home to her classroom behavior that day. This is typically done by developing a "behavior contract" between student, parent, and teacher.

THE BEHAVIOR CONTRACT

Although the details will differ, behavior contracts basically involve two steps: first, specifying the behavior that is to be rewarded; and second, following through with a positive and/or negative consequence, depending on whether or not the child meets the conditions of the contract.

Many teachers use behavior contracts in their classroom as a matter of routine. For example, they will write a child's name on the board, or use some type of demerit system, if a student is doing something inappropriate. If a child's name does not appear on the board more than a certain number of times in a week, she wins some special privilege on Friday, such as getting to perform a highly valued activity (using a computer, playing a game, or being allowed to select a fun book to read). While such systems are usually set up for the entire class, sometimes a teacher will design an in-class contract specifically for one child.

When a teacher's efforts fail to motivate a child to conform to appropriate classroom behavior, a behavior contract coordinated between school and home can be most helpful. A simple example of such a contract for a younger child might involve a colored card system. Let's say the targeted behavior is a child's uncooperativeness. If Susie has a great day and is highly cooperative, the teacher will send her home with a green card. A so-so day will result in a yellow card, and a very problematic day will earn the red card.

When the child comes home with the card, her evening privileges depend upon the color she receives: A green card entitles her to some special privilege (a thirty-minute-later bedtime, having the dog sleep in her room, watching a favorite video, or playing a video game for thirty minutes); a yellow card earns her a normal evening, without special privilege or negative consequence; a red card results in her receiving a negative consequence (no television that night, an earlier bedtime, or no playing outside after school).

In order for this system to work, it is critical that the privileges the child can earn are really special to her. Consequently, the child must be included in the contract planning. The system can be strengthened even more by offering some type of weekly incentive. For example, if a youngster receives no red cards during the week, she's allowed to do a previously agreed-upon weekend activity that would not occur if she hadn't had a red-card-free week.

Of course, there are many variations of this general plan. Some teachers prefer to use a two-card system. Or instead of cards, the teacher might stamp or draw a "smiling" versus "frowning" face on the back of a child's hand, or on one of her papers.

For an older child, a check-plus, check, and check-minus system can be used instead of cards and faces. Some older youngsters will respond well to a *weekly* reporting system rather than needing daily reinforcement.

The point is that the child receives a consistent message from parents and teacher alike that school behavior is important. Once the youngster has improved her behavior for a grading period, she can be "graduated" from the contract. If her behavior slips, the contract can be started again.

With younger elementary-school children, a contract will usually be more successful if it is used on a daily basis. Once behavior improves, the child can be switched to a weekly contract in which the teacher gives a report to the parent at the end of each school week.

Although contracts are probably used most often for a child's conduct problems, they are also helpful in getting a child to complete and return his homework (see Chapter 7), and for a child's being tardy, forgetting necessary books and supplies, reading magazines in class, etc.

COMMON PROBLEM SITUATIONS

THE CHILD WHO WON'T SIT STILL

Kenneth is having problems staying in his seat at school. He finds every excuse to sharpen his pencil or roam around the room. When he is seated, he's usually moving or fidgeting.

When your child has this problem, you (or the teacher) might be tempted to jump to the conclusion that he has a condition known as Attention Deficit Disorder with Hyperactivity (often called ADDH). While you might be right, such a diagnosis can be made only after careful evaluation. Typically, this will include both teacher and parent filling out a specially designed rating scale containing questions about the child's daily behavior, as well as formal educational, psychological, neurological, and/or psychiatric evaluations (for more information, see Chapter 9).

You might ask, "Why else would a child be so restless if he's not hyperactive?" Common reasons might include boredom, excessive anxiety, oppositionality, and allergic reactions. Obviously, appropriate treatment for the child will depend upon addressing the underlying problem.

Also, youngsters just starting school might simply be reflecting a parenting style in which the youngster has few limits set on his behavior. If this is the case, the problem can be eliminated by parents learning effective child management skills.

Realize that it can be difficult to draw an objective line between a child who simply has a high activity level and the child who is truly hyperactive. Some youngsters, called kinesthetic learners (for more information, see Chapter 9) actually need to move about in order to learn. A parent or teacher who is unaware of this fact, and who sets very strict standards about what is considered "inappropriate" movement, may overreact in thinking that such a child is hyperactive.

If evaluation does reveal that a youngster is hyperactive, treatment usually involves counseling for the parents in behavior management and/or medication for the child. Some parents have made changes in their child's diet which have been helpful, although other parents have tried this approach and have not seen any change in their child's activity level. Obviously, the method of treatment is a personal decision to be made by parents after consulting with their pediatrician and/or other medical and mental-health consultants.

Classroom management might also include a behavior contract in which "staying on task" would be the target behavior. This term would be defined for your child as doing whatever he is asked to do without disturbing his classmates, paying attention, and controlling his impulses to wander about or engage in behavior that is unrelated to his assignment.

THE "CLASS CLOWN"

Danny is constantly clowning around in school. He'll do almost anything to get a laugh from his peers, and he is getting in trouble in school for his silliness and his wisecracking.

While some "class clowns" are well liked by their peers, many times such a child remains on the fringe of his peer group. Although he does get *attention* from his classmates, he often remains friendless. In such cases, his clowning may stem from low self-esteem due to anxiety about his acceptance by his peers and/or about his lack of academic success (many such children have learning problems). Also, he may be using his inappropriate bids for attention as an expression of underlying anger. Rather than being defiant, argumentative, or openly aggressive, he rebels by goofing off and acting silly.

If a behavior contract is used, the target would be "appropriate behavior." This would be defined for him as not engaging in silly behavior and not making wisecracks while the teacher is talking or when the class is supposed to be working on an assignment.

If your child responds well to a behavior contract and discontinues his clowning, you may need to do nothing further. He simply needs a little extra structure to control his impulses. However, if he shows other signs of low self-esteem, rebellion, or inability to make friends, or if he has underlying learning difficulties, you'll also want to address these problems. If your efforts seem unsuccessful, it's wise to consult a mental-health professional.

HAVING TO BE FIRST

Ellen looks at every activity as a competition. She wants to be first in line, first to finish her class work, first to have the latest fad in clothing, and first to answer a question in class. When she can't be "first," she either argues or pouts.

Certainly, you'll want to talk with Ellen about her behavior. Let her know that it is unrealistic for anyone to be first in everything. Being first is a nice accomplishment in the case of a structured competition, such as a race or a contest. However, all the other people who aren't first are not failures, and may in fact have performed very well.

Explain to Ellen that, rather than impressing her peers with her behavior, she's actually likely to alienate them. Taking turns or allowing others to be first is important for social success. Kids, as with adults, like people who are considerate of other people's feelings. If a person always has to be first, this automatically means that she always wants her friends to be second! Also, ask Ellen to put herself in her classmates' shoes by imagining how she would feel if someone else never let *her* have a chance to be first.

In addition to talking with your daughter about the effects of her behavior, you'll also want to think about *why* she needs to behave the way she does. The bid to be first is a bid for attention, possibly combined with impulsiveness and an inability to wait. You'll need to make sure that she gets plenty of attention in positive ways, and that you begin praising her for showing patience and consideration for other people by taking her turn rather than racing to be first.

If a behavior contract is used in the classroom, the target behaviors would be "taking necessary time to do work" and "taking turns with other people."

HAVING TO WIN

Harvey is getting in trouble in school because he hates to lose. Whether it's a spelling bee, a class nomination, or just a game on the playground, he *has* to win. When he doesn't, he challenges the rules, argues about unfairness, and/or walks away in disgust, refusing to participate any longer.

Just as with the child who always wants to be first, you would need to expain to Harvey the negative results that his behavior causes with his peers. Kids think that a child who always has to win is stuck-up, and they make fun of sore losers.

But how do you get to the root of a child's need to win? Have you emphasized achievement too much, giving him the impression that the only way he can win your approval is by achieving? Or perhaps you or the other parent are very competitive, or one or both of you are very high achievers. Your son could be modeling your behavior in spite of the fact that you're not emphasizing that *he* achieve. If so, you'll need to tell him that your love for him isn't based on his ability to achieve. Show him that you really mean this by giving him praise for his other personal qualities (sense of humor, consideration for other people, helpfulness, creativity, etc.) in addition to praise for his achievements.

Perhaps your child is very competitive because he's jealous of a brother or sister, and he's trying to gain your favor by being "better" than his sibling. If you think this is the case, ask him directly if he thinks you prefer another sibling to him. Then reassure him that you love each of your children in a special way, pointing out his qualities that endear him to you. Let him know that he is totally unique since there is no other person in the world just like him. Therefore, he doesn't have to compete with anyone for your love; he already has it.

Also, ask yourself if you could be unintentionally encouraging your child to feel entitled to special privileges. Do you bend to his wishes too much, allowing him to control things at home? Such a situation is especially likely to occur with an only child. Having no other children to consider, many parents of an only child fall into the habit of allowing the child to determine where to eat out, what television program to watch, or where to go on weekends. Parents don't realize that in giving their child so much power, they're setting up the youngster to expect to get his way in all circumstances.

If this is the case, begin to show your child that he's not omnipotent by insisting that you or the other parent make some of the decisions you've been leaving up to him. Of course, you'll let him make the decision *some* of the time, but insisting that your preferences be taken into account teaches him the need to consider other people's feelings and wishes.

The target behavior in a classroom contract for the child who has to win would be "remaining positive (or being a good sport) when someone else wins."

REFUSING TO WORK INDEPENDENTLY

The teacher tells you that Allison wants her constant attention. Allison refuses to do her work unless the teacher gives her continual feedback, and often comes up to the teacher's desk with an unnecessary question. She doesn't get her work done unless she receives this one-on-one attention.

There are several possible reasons Allison might be having this need for so much individual attention from the teacher. Does Allison have a vision or hearing problem? Many youngsters don't have vision or hearing screenings done in their preschool years, so this possibility needs to be ruled out.

It might be that the work is actually too difficult for Allison. She may have an undiagnosed learning difference which makes it difficult for her to understand verbal or written instructions, or to understand the actual subject matter. This would be less likely if she _easily_ does the work when the teacher is with her _without_ the teacher reinterpreting the instructions or assisting her with answers. If a possible learning difficulty is suspected, Allison should have a diagnostic evaluation.

Could Allison's behavior with the teacher reflect a general overdependence? Is she accustomed to having someone's total attention at home, and has not learned to do things for herself? If this is the case, you'll want to make some changes. If she's not already doing so, make sure she's dressing and bathing herself, and that she has some age-appropriate responsibilities (picking up toys, carrying her meal dishes from the table to the kitchen counter, giving water to the cat, or setting the table). Be sure she's learned to sleep in her own bed at night, and that she spends some time during the day occupying herself and not having your undivided attention.

Is it possible that Allison is carrying out typical responsibilities for her age *except* in the area of homework? Has she specifically decided to use learning tasks as a way to get an adult's total attention at home? If so, begin to wean her from having to have an adult present when she does homework (see Chapter 7).

Also, consider whether or not Allison's behavior might reflect a high level of anxiety. Does she have many fears and insecurities, feeling afraid if she is not in close physical proximity to an adult? Consultation with a mental health professional would be helpful in pinpointing the origin of this difficulty.

Could it be that something traumatic happening at home is making Allison temporarily more dependent on adult attention? Examples might be a recent divorce, illness of a parent or grandparent, or any other situation in which a child might feel that she will be or has been abandoned by an important person in her life. If so, she'll need appropriate reassurance.

Perhaps she doesn't feel free to ask the questions she has about what's going on and, in your attempt to protect her, you haven't honestly addressed the real issues with her. Actually, you will help her more by telling her the truth and by encouraging her to ask questions than by trying to shield her with silence. Children can handle the truth far better than the uncertainty of the unknown, and will feel reassured just by knowing they can trust their parents to tell them what's really going on.

While the underlying cause of Allison's overdependence obviously needs to be addressed, a behavior contract in the classroom can be helpful. The target behavior would be to "work independently," which would be explained to Allison as including staying in her seat, and not going up to the teacher's desk to ask questions that have already been explained.

THE STUBBORN CHILD

While Ian is never defiant or disruptive, he's the kind of child who will only do what *he* wants to do, *when* he wants to do it. When he decides to be cooperative, he does fine. The problem is, how do you get him to *want* to be cooperative?

Ian's method of stubbornly refusing to cooperate is a form of passive aggression. In other words, he doesn't overtly argue with you about doing something you've asked of him. He just quietly refuses to do it. Such a child can sometimes be even more frustrating than the youngster who is outright rebellious!

If your child is being stubborn only at school, try to find out what is upsetting him to the point that he's being so uncooperative. Is he angry with the teacher? Is he bored with his classwork? Is he upset with one of his classmates?

Chances are, however, that a child who demonstrates passive aggressive behavior in the classroom also shows the same kind of reactions at home. If so, you need to ask yourself how you might have been inadvertently reinforcing this pattern of behavior. A common way is for a parent to give a child certain tasks (such as chores), nag him repeatedly to get them done, but then do nothing to get the child to follow through. Instead of putting effort into nagging (and giving the youngster so much attention for what he's *not* doing), it would be better to set a negative consequence for him until he complies with your request.

Some children also become passive aggressive in reaction to parents who are overly controlling, not giving the youngster any say-so in the decisions that affect him. Certainly, it's not that a parent should give a child carte blanche to do whatever he wishes. But kids do need to express their opinions and to learn how to think for themselves. If parents don't allow them to have such choices about age-appropriate decisions, those parents are being overly controlling. The response of the child might be to "dig in" and express his anger passively via stubborness and covert uncooperation.

Passive aggressive behavior can also occur when parents don't allow a child to express anger directly. Children need to learn *appropriate* ways to vent their angry feelings (see "Excessive Aggression" later in this chapter for ideas). When appropriate expression of anger is forbidden, a youngster may react with passive measures which are most irritating.

For the stubborn child in the classroom, a behavior contract would target "working consistently in class" as the desired behavior.

"STIRRING UP" CLASSMATES

Nathan is continually encouraging his classmates to get involved in misbehavior. He eggs on other children who are involved in conflict, makes sarcastic remarks, and generally encourages rebellion in the classroom.

Realize that although Nathan gets into trouble with teachers by behaving in this manner, he may be seen as "cool" or heroic to his peers. Even if his misbehavior does not bring admiration or envy from his classmates, he's still likely to get a feeling of power for his ability to cause disruption.

As with any child who is being rebellious, either actively or passively, it's important to address the underlying causes. Is he reacting to a family problem? Is he feeling inadequate academically, socially, or personally? Does he have a diagnosable attention or impulse disorder (see Chapter 9)? Is he responding to a stressful or traumatic circumstance? Is there someone whom he admires (father, big brother, a high-status peer, television hero) who encourages him to act macho or to be a rebel?

Remember that, especially in children, anger and rebellion often mask underlying feelings of depression. Unless you are successful in figuring out the source of your child's rebelliousness and are able to see quick progress in his behavior, seek professional counseling to assist you and the child.

Of course, the rebellious child needs a clear, consistent message at home and at school that such behavior is unacceptable. A behavior contract targeting "cooperative behavior" would be appropriate.

CHEATING

Arnie comes home from school with a sad face and a note from his teacher. He's been caught cheating on a test.

First, let Arnie know that you realize it must have been hard for him to give you this bad news, and you appreciate his giving you the note. Many children tear up or hide such notes from their parents, and you can praise him for his honesty.

Then address the cheating issue with him. Try to establish his motivation by asking him what he thinks would have happened if he *hadn't* cheated. Typically, he'll tell you that he was afraid he wouldn't do well on the test because he didn't study or because he didn't understand the material. Ask him, "And then what do you think would have happened if you'd failed the test or gotten a low grade?" Probably he'll answer that he was afraid you would be angry with him and/or would give him some negative consequence for his behavior.

Explain to your child that you would always prefer him to make a low grade honestly than to make a higher one by cheating. Then tell him what you *would* do if he got a low grade. For example, if he had not been doing and turning in his homework, you might limit his television viewing in the evenings until he brought the grade up, or you might set up a designated study period for him until you see that he could manage his time more wisely. If he had been putting effort into the subject but still had trouble understanding it, you might arrange for him to get special help from the teacher before or after class, if possible, or get him a tutor.

Reassure him that although you might be angry with him for letting his assignments slide, it would not be the end of the world. You would want him to learn from his mistake, but not to beat himself up over it. Be sure to tell him directly that, even though you want him to do well in school, your love for him is not based on what kind of grades he makes.

In all probability, the teacher already will have given your child a consequence for his cheating, probably a zero on his test. You really don't need to do anything further if this is his first instance of cheating, other than to follow through with what you've already explained to him would happen when he makes a low grade. Let him know that you expect that he has learned from his mistake and will not repeat it, rather than lecturing him on the evils of cheating or threatening him with dire consequences should he ever do it again.

But what if your child obviously sees nothing wrong with

cheating, telling you that "everybody does it, so why can't I?" Let him know that you realize some children do choose to cheat, and that they may not even get caught for a while. However, the cheater only cheats himself. Not only does he miss out on learning and understanding the material, but he also has to deal with the guilty conscience that comes from being deceitful. Also, if a cheater keeps cheating, he almost always gets caught.

If your child repeats the situation by continuing to cheat, consultation with a mental health professional would be recommended.

ARGUING

The teacher calls to tell you that Chris will not accept instruction or limits in class. He argues with her constantly.

If you receive this complaint from a teacher, chances are, you're not totally surprised. The youngster who argues in school is also likely to be the kind of child who always tries to have the "last word" at home. But what do you do now that his argumentativeness is creating problems in school?

The easiest way to control this problem in the classroom is to set up a behavior contract that targets "following instructions without arguing" as the desired behavior. In order to deal with the real issue, however, some changes will need to be made at home.

What is likely is that the child has learned that by arguing, he can often manipulate a parent into giving him his way. Even if the parent doesn't wear down and give him what he wants, he has still gotten extra attention through the arguing process. And kids, when given the choice, will always opt for getting negative attention rather than *no* attention at all.

Also, realize that a child can't have an argument with himself. The parent must be arguing back, or there would be no discussion! Parents can get caught up in arguing because they believe that they must demonstrate their parental control by having the last word. But in actuality, the last word means *nothing*. It is the parent's leverage over the child that shows control, not the number of words uttered, or who talks last. Since parents set the rules and dispense privileges for children, they have all the leverage they need.

So it's okay to let the child utter those last words. The youngster is simply attempting to save face by issuing the last retort, and a parent is wise to ignore it *unless* the remark is clearly off limits (the child calls you a vulgar name, or curses at you). Even if the latter occurs, your response would be to set another negative consequence for such inappropriate behavior, not to argue about what the child actually said.

The other point to realize about arguing is that it can represent what is called a "polarity response." The parent says it's cold, so the child argues that it's hot. In other words, the child always takes the *opposite* position to what the parent has stated. Parents often set themselves up for this kind of response by being too "parental" or authoritarian. That is, they issue orders and make demands, tell a child what he should or should not feel, and attempt to exert excessive control over him. They don't take his feelings and thoughts into account, insisting on strict obedience without any questioning.

While some children will deal with this type of parent by becoming passive and acquiescent, other children will develop a polarity response. Power struggles and arguing will result. In such cases, the polarity response actually represents the child's attempt to preserve his right to decide some things for himself.

If you think your child has developed a polarity response, begin to find ways to show him that you do respect his ideas and feelings. Allow him to make his own choices whenever it is appropriate. Even if you end up insisting that he do something he doesn't want to do, at least hear him out about his reasons for thinking differently. He may have a good point that you have overlooked.

EXCESSIVE AGGRESSION

Mark is continually getting into disputes with his classmates. He seems to provoke other kids with his aggressive remarks and bad temper. Now the teacher has called to tell you that he's starting fights on the playground.

When a child is overly aggressive, it is most likely to be from one of two causes. Either he is getting the message that such behavior is desirable, or he is feeling very angry inside (although he might not be conscious of it).

In the first case, a child might be trying to cover up inner feelings of inferiority by acting tough or macho. He thinks that behaving aggressively demonstrates his masculinity and braveness. Even some girls will put on a tough facade, thinking it is "cool."

Sometimes, children will model the aggressive behavior of their parents, or of television heroes. If exposed to an environment where violence or aggression is common, the child will conform. Of course, some children live in neighborhoods or belong to subcultures where aggressiveness is highly valued, or even a necessary survival skill. The reputation for "not backing down" and for having the bravado to fight represents a high mark of status in such groups. Such a child may end up in a school that is made up of youngsters from a different culture, and may find that his aggressive behavior is not valued by the new group.

If a child has learned to value aggressiveness, for whatever reason, he needs to be given clear guidelines about what is to be expected in school. Parents need to support the school's position that such aggressive behavior is not appropriate in school, and give him the clear message that they value solving problems by negotiating and compromising. Children need to be told directly that there are times when they will not get their way, even if they are correct or have a good idea, and that accepting another's choice is usually preferred to escalating a disagreement into a fight. An exception to this would be a situation where a youngster can successfully step in to physically stop another child from hurting a peer, or from being cruel to an animal.

If a child is being aggressive because he is angry, you'll want to determine the source of the anger. There are many reasons why a child might be angry, including intense sibling rivalry, overcoercive parenting, reaction to feelings of being abandoned (such as death of a loved one, or one parent moving away), physical or sexual abuse, feelings that he can't please a parent, unfair treatment at home or at school, or learning problems. Sometimes professional counseling may be necessary to get to the root of the child's problem.

Appropriate Ways to Express Anger

Whatever the reasons for the child's anger, he'll need to be instructed in appropriate ways to release that anger. Parents are usually quite good about explaining what a child should *not* do when he's angry (hit, kick, spit, yell, throw things, or destroy property), but they frequently don't tell a youngster what he *can* do about these feelings.

Tell your child that he can show his anger to his peers by forcefully saying things like "I'm mad!" or "I don't like that!" or "I won't play with you anymore if you keep doing that!" Let him know that he can release anger through some physical activity, such as kicking a ball or riding his bike. Some youngsters like to draw angry pictures to illustrate what is making them angry. Others like to have something to punch, kick, or throw (a pillow, rag doll, or stuffed animal). Some children like the idea of having a private cassette tape on which they can record any angry message, saying anything they'd *like* to say in person, but shouldn't. (In order for this option to work, the child needs to know that this tape is private, and nobody will listen to it without his permission.)

Many elementary-school children like to use a "mad bag" to release their angry feelings. This can be made by stuffing a canvas bag with old clothing or rags. The bag should be big enough for the child to straddle, but not so big that he can't throw it around. When he's angry, he lets the bag represent whatever or whomever he's upset with, pounding, kicking, or throwing it until his anger is released.

Whether a youngster is aggressive because of his learning experience or because of inner anger, it's helpful to limit his watching television shows and movies that model aggressive or violent behavior. Such viewing can stir up his aggressive fantasies, and can give the message that you condone the behavior that is being shown.

Using a behavior contract in the classroom to help a child control his aggressive impulses can be very helpful. In this case, the targeted behavior would be "cooperating," which would include getting along with peers and expressing anger appropriately.

CHALLENGING THE TEACHER

The teacher reports that Kelly is very disrespectful in class. Kelly talks back, and makes challenging remarks such as, "You can't tell me what to do!"

Since rudeness can be an expression of anger or rebellion, you would want to consider the same issues that you would address with the overly aggressive child (see previous entry). However, there is another possibility to consider, not having anything to do with excessive anger.

Kelly may react the way she does because of a pattern of communication that has developed at home. You might be a parent who values individual expression and encourages your child to state her opinions on most matters. You may consider her to be a "free spirit," and are fearful of stunting her intellectual growth and creativity by setting too many limits. If Kelly is bright and articulate, you might be quite liberal about allowing her to challenge you, to debate household issues, and to express herself bluntly. Unfortunately, this parental stance tends to set up a youngster for future authority conflicts.

The problem arises when Kelly has to deal with other adults, especially teachers, who must set rules for the benefit of a group of children, rather than for just one child. In a class of twenty or thirty youngsters, not every child can freely express her opinion on every event and on what the teacher should or shouldn't do.

If you think this situation applies to Kelly, have a talk with her about the appropriate way to relate to a teacher. Let her know that challenging remarks to teachers are rude, and that there are some things only grown-ups are allowed to decide. While it is true that no one, including a teacher, can *make* her do anything, you expect her to follow class rules, even if she doesn't agree with them. Reassure her that she will have plenty of opportunities to express her thoughts in writing assignments and in class discussions where opinions are invited.

Again, a behavior contract can be used to reduce classroom rudeness. The target behavior would be "reacting appropriately and cooperatively with the teacher."

CHAPTER 6

When Achievement Becomes an Issue

MOST PARENTS HAVE STRONG OPINIONS ABOUT WHAT KIND OF grades their children should make in school. Some will expect report cards consisting mostly of A's, especially if their child is bright. Some will be pleased so long as their youngster makes nothing lower than a C. Others will consider C's to be inappropriate, even though technically, a C is an average grade. And a few are just concerned that their child will pass.

Where a parent sets the criteria for acceptable achievement can depend a great deal on that parent's personal history. The parent who slid along with mediocre grades in school but who is very successful as an adult might not be as uptight about his youngster's grades as the parent who blames his lack of success on the fact that he didn't put forth much effort in school.

How a parent's *parents* reacted to his own school achievement can also color that parent's expectations for his own child. If he feels that he was unduly pressured throughout school, he might vow to bend over backward *not* to push his own child. On the other hand, the parent who feels that his parents didn't care *enough* about his performance in school might decide that he will help his child most by setting very high achievement goals for the youngster.

Whatever the parents' expectations, trouble can occur when a child's level of achievement falls short of what a parent considers to be appropriate. If the cause of a child's poor performance turns out to be because he is intellectually limited, or perhaps very average, a parent can feel painful disappointment. Yet it can be just as disappointing if the parent discovers that a youngster is extremely bright, but is showing only mediocre achievement.

Of course, parents aren't the only ones with expectations. There are youngsters who push themselves to make 100's when their parents would be perfectly content with B's or C's. But whether it is the parent or the child who needs to adjust his academic goals, emotions can run high when there is a discrepancy between expectation and performance.

FACTORS THAT CAN AFFECT YOUR CHILD'S ACHIEVEMENT

A number of factors, operating separately or together, can affect a child's performance in school.

Physical Factors

Obviously, a child's school performance will require adequate vision and hearing, and many public schools and pediatricians routinely screen youngsters to determine if further evaluation is necessary. If your child develops problems with her schoolwork, you'll want to be sure to rule out the possibility that she has a vision or hearing loss. Also, many times youngsters who normally hear well can have fluid in their ears after an ear infection, and cannot properly discriminate sounds until the fluid is gone.

Another physical factor has to do with whether or not a child is getting adequate sleep. If your daughter sleeps fitfully or doesn't develop a regular sleep pattern, consult your pediatrician about the possible cause. If she's groggy in the mornings or falls asleep later in the day, try giving her an earlier bedtime.

Whether or not a child has had breakfast can also make a difference in her ability to function well in school. If she's hungry, her performance can suffer.

Obviously, a child who has an illness will not be able to do her best in school. Even if she's not sick enough to stay home, as is the case with many children who have allergy and/or sinus problems, her physical symptoms can be bothersome enough to create concentration problems.

Another very important physical factor is a child's neurological organization, or brain functioning. Some children's brains simply work differently from the majority, although still considered to be within normal range. These children may experience problems with establishing a clear hand preference (right- or left-handedness). They frequently are highly distractible and have difficulty controlling their impulses. Some have seizures, which may or may not manifest in an obvious way, but which can be seen when brain waves are monitored. Such youngsters are considered to be at higher risk for various learning difficulties.

Environmental Factors

A child must be comfortable if he is to learn most effectively. Things like classroom temperature, adequate ventilation, noise level (in and outside of the classroom), lighting, and how he fits in his seat or desk can affect his comfort level. Clothing that is too tight or scratchy can also interfere with a youngster's ability to concentrate.

Intellectual Capability

Other things being equal, the brighter child will usually learn more quickly than the very average child. And if a youngster is below average in ability, he'll typically learn more slowly than will his classmate who is average.

However, parents often overrate the influence of a child's intellectual capability. Given a certain minimum level of intelligence, a child's actual achievement is very dependent on his level of motivation and effort. The very average child who is persevering and hardworking may end up with a college degree, while a gifted youngster may drop out of high school because of a lack of sufficient motivation. Also, a stimulating environment will nurture intellectual development; this is why parents are encouraged to read to their young children, to take them to interesting places, to discuss concepts and ideas with them, and to encourage them to have an inquisitive attitude. (For information about assessment of intelligence, see Chapter 9.)

Family Factors

Children who are experiencing traumatic situations at home will often show a drop in their performance in school. The birth of a sibling, marital discord, a divorce, an illness or death of a significant person in the child's life, physical or sexual abuse, an older sibling's leaving home, or a parent's emotional problems can trigger a child's regression in the classroom. Once the child has been helped to work through or adjust to the traumatic event, his performance will usually return to its former level.

Emotional Factors

Children, like adults, can suffer from anxiety and depression. They may develop specific fears, show poor self-esteem, have physical ailments related to emotional causes, exhibit mood swings, manifest compulsive behavior rituals, and so on. Obviously, these and other emotional factors can interfere with a child's ability to learn.

Behavior Problems

Youngsters who are overly aggressive, oppositional, defiant, excessively silly, or who show other behaviors inappropriate to the classroom usually come into conflict with their teachers. Such behaviors require energy, resulting in a child's not being able to put consistent energy into learning.

Motivational Factors

Children who are unmotivated to learn in school can be a difficult challenge to the most competent and creative teacher. By contrast, youngsters who are eager to learn will learn in spite of less-than-optimal learning conditions. Of course, a child's level of motivation can be affected by many factors, including feelings about his capabilities, his relationship with his parents and siblings, stress in his environment, trauma, his social relationships, and his experiences in school.

HOW DO YOU MEASURE ACHIEVEMENT?

The report card is only one measure of a child's achievement. Specific grades are supposed to reflect a child's performance in various subjects, but they *can* be more a measure of a teacher's generosity (or lack of it) than a measure of a child's achievement. In special-education classes, grades often are more a measure of effort than of actual achievement, since a child receiving an A in special education might get a D or F for the same work if he were in a mainstream class. The point is, report-card grades reflect the subjective opinion of a teacher.

Standardized Tests

The other measure of how well a child is learning is the standardized achievement test. These tests compare a child's performance with that of same-aged peers (often both nationally and at the local level) in a variety of school subjects. While objectively scored, they still may not accurately reflect a child's actual abilities. Such tests are usually administered in a group situation, so the possibility of a child's cheating exists. Even more common, a child might not feel well or might have some situational problem the day the test is given, and will make a low score which is inaccurate. Some youngsters are also poor testers, becoming highly anxious under the pressure of timed tests.

Obviously, the best scenario occurs when a child's report card grades and achievement test scores send the same message. Parents might be surprised and confused when this is not the case. They might become angry, feeling misled by the teacher's grading, if a child has been getting high marks on a report card but then turns up with mediocre scores on an achievement test. Or they might deny the low achievement test scores, believing that their child just had a bad day on the day of testing.

Equally distressing to parents is the case in which the child scores high on achievement tests, but makes average or low grades in school. Assuming the teacher is a fair grader, this suggests that the child is underachieving for some reason. Parents typically use such scores to point out to their child that he is capable of making much higher grades and that he is not living up to his academic potential.

The message you give your child about his performance on his report card and on achievement tests will not only tell what your expectations are for him in school, but it can also affect his self-esteem. It's important to youngsters that you take the time to consider carefully the information you've been given. A child who has done well will certainly want your praise; a child who has done poorly needs to know that you still support him and that you will give him practical suggestions on how he can improve.

Motivating with Understanding

The problem is that many parents, in their eagerness to motivate a child to bring up a low grade or score, immediately focus on every aspect of the report card that is negative. They'll say nothing about the score that went *up* from the last grading period, but will jump on the one that went *down*. Or they'll neglect to mention the A's and B's, but will ask the child to explain how he ended up with a C. Or they'll ignore a child's good grades to complain about his lower conduct marks, or vice versa.

By focusing first on the negative, parents can cause a child to feel that he can never please the most important people in his life. If a child is given the message that *he* is a big disappointment, or if he feels excessively criticized, he can become filled with anxiety about his inadequacies, develop a defensive "who cares, anyway" attitude about schoolwork, or express his anger in rebellious behavior.

Whatever problems your child's report cards or test scores reveal, discuss the situation calmly and matter-of-factly with him. Comment first on whatever positive things are evident. Then say something like "I see you're having some problems in math class" or, for a generally poor report card, "Looks like you had some troubles this grading period. What do you think went wrong?" If your child made all A's except for one B or C, resist the temptation to say something like "Why on earth did you get that B?" or "Gee, you'd have all A's if it wasn't for that B!" If you must bring up the lower mark, try saying something like "How do you feel about getting the B in social studies?" or "Were you disappointed about getting a B?" This invites your youngster to give you important information, and doesn't imply criticism or disappointment.

Before telling your son what measures you will take to help him improve his grades or scores, ask him if *he* has any ideas about how to correct the problems he's having. He might suggest that he begin his homework right after he gets home from school, that he will go to before-school tutoring, or that he will not watch so much television in the evenings. If he has a good idea, help him convert it into a concrete plan. If your son can't think of any ways he might help himself to get better marks, go ahead and tell him how you think he can improve, setting up a concrete plan with him.

Refrain from having a temper tantrum about your child's report card, or from giving your child lengthy lectures about how he'll need to bring up his grades if he's ever going to amount to anything. This behavior really doesn't help solve the problem, and it can actually make matters worse. If you have difficulty controlling your emotions, it helps to remind yourself that this particular event won't seem terribly important when your child is thirty!

College Aside

Many parents appeal to a child to put more effort into making good grades by telling him that he must do so in order to get into a good college when he's older. While there are many reasons why you want your youngster to do well in elementary school (to build a knowledge base, to acquire skills in reading, writing, and math that might be necessary in his job or career as an adult, to build his sense of confidence and capability, and to have an educated perspective about his world), concerns about college should not be one of them. You probably want him to like learning and to find school a positive experience so that he will want to continue his education as far as his capabilities will allow.

The truth is that grades in elementary school are not even *known* when a youngster applies to college! Many youngsters who perform at a mediocre level in the early school years actually end up doing well in college. So you can take the pressure off *yourself* about the implications of your child's elementary-school grades on his getting into college.

By trying to motivate your youngster to do better in school by thinking about college when he's in grade school, you also risk setting up the expectation that if he isn't a top student, he might as well give up on the notion of college. If he's in a power struggle with you about his school achievement, he might even rebel against your well-intentioned pressure by deciding that he won't even *consider* going to college, since it's so important to you!

COMMON PROBLEM SITUATIONS

NOT LIVING UP TO POTENTIAL

David consistently scores in the gifted range on achievement tests. Both you and his teachers tell him that he is capable of being a superior student, and that he has a great future ahead of him. But David seems totally unmotivated to work in school, putting forth only the minimal effort he needs just to barely pass.

Begin by talking to your child about his apparent lack of interest in his schoolwork. Ask him why he thinks it "doesn't matter," as his answer might give you a useful clue. However, many times such an unmotivated youngster will not really know why he's unmotivated, or will give you an excuse, such as "It's stupid," or "It's too much trouble."

Unless you're lucky enough to have a son who will give you

a bona fide reason for his lack of motivation, you'll want to explore every avenue to help him perform up to his level of capability. First, ask your pediatrician or family doctor to evaluate him, making sure that a physical problem isn't contributing to the difficulty. You will also want to determine if he is sleeping well, since many youngsters who have trouble falling asleep or staying asleep neglect to mention this fact to their parents.

Is it possible that your child is simply bored with school? If his classwork is too easy, he may see no point in doing what he sees as "busy work." If he says he is bored, ask his teacher to give him more challenging assignments, and enroll him in enrichment activities in your community that will stimulate his intellectual development.

Also, consider whether or not a family problem is contributing to your child's lack of success in school. Is he angry with you, perhaps unconsciously, and is his lack of achievement his way to get back at you? Is he feeling lonely at home and is using this means to get some extra attention from you? Is he depressed? Is he having some other emotional or social problem that causes him to remain unmotivated?

You can also try to improve your child's motivation with a behavior contract at home, negotiating to give him specific privileges in return for his bringing up his grades to an acceptable level. For example, his good effort in school each week could be rewarded by some weekend privilege, by money to be saved up for video games, or by allowing him to earn game time on the family computer. Of course, you can also have a contract specifying negative consequences for your child's lack of cooperation in school. For example, you might remove a prized computer, radio, or television from his room and have him earn it back by improving his school performance.

If you're not successful in helping your child to function closer to his potential, you might be tempted to take a hands-off approach and let *him* take full responsibility for his schoolwork and grades (given that you've tried everything else). This is a reasonable solution for a high-school student. An elementary-school student, however, is too young to take on this responsibility. Consult a mental health professional to get advice if the situation doesn't improve.

REPEATING A GRADE

Bob has always had difficulty with school. Now in fifth grade, his effort is minimal and his grades continue to border on failing. The school has asked you to consider the possibility of having Bob repeat fifth grade.

There are many factors to consider in making the important decision about whether or not a youngster should repeat a grade. These include his current achievement level, his social maturity, his physical size, and how much school he's missed in the current year.

Kids whose academic skills (reading, writing, math) are *below* grade level and who are physically small and/or socially immature will probably be very comfortable repeating a grade. The same is true for children who are behind academically and who have missed a good deal of school due to illness, repeated family moves, or similar upheavals. To promote these youngsters to the next grade would subject them to a struggle to keep up with their peers, both academically and socially.

However, there are many children who score below grade level in one or more skills because of diagnosable learning problems, yet they are socially and physically compatible with their peer group. In addition, there are youngsters who continue to achieve at or above grade level, but who make failing grades due to a lack of motivation or to an uncooperative attitude.

If such a youngster is in kindergarten (discussed in Chapter 2) or first grade, repeating a grade might be helpful. These young children are not as susceptible to the self-esteem problems that older children can suffer as a result of repeating a grade, so long as parents clearly and matter-of-factly present the positive reasons why they want a child to repeat a grade: for example, "This was a hard year for you because of———, so we want you to be in first grade another year so it will make the rest of elementary school much easier and happier for you." For second grade and above, however, students usually will benefit more by receiving specific kinds of help rather than by being retained.

The child with learning difficulties can participate in many types of public school special education programs (for more information, see Chapter 9). He also often can take advantage of tutoring and other special academic programs offered in most communities during the summer. Consequently, he usually can be kept in the same grade as his age-mates and still receive the special academic help he needs.

Youngsters who are unmotivated or uncooperative will usually not be helped by keeping them back a grade. In fact, this tactic often only reinforces their negative feelings about school, worsening the situation. Yet parents, in their understandable frustration, often think that this type of child should have to repeat a grade to suffer the consequence of not doing his work. However, a youngster can be given *other* consequences (attending summer school, loss of privileges, etc.), rather than being punished ineffectively by retention.

What the uncooperative or unmotivated child really needs is for his parents to understand the root cause of his negativism. He could have a diagnosable emotional problem, or it could be that he simply is not receiving parental attention or support regarding school. Either way, parents need to address the issue, probably including counseling for both the child and his family.

Realize that the above statements are meant to be *general* recommendations only. The issue of whether or not a particular child should be held back a grade depends on the complicated combination of many factors, and should be decided on an individual basis.

BOOSTING SELF-ESTEEM IN THE LOW ACHIEVER

Brandy has to work hard in school to make very average grades. As fate would have it, her best friend and her older sister are A students who find schoolwork to be easy. You're concerned because Brandy is starting to make remarks that suggest she's not feeling very good about herself.

You'll want to make the point to Brandy that grades are not the only measure of a person's worth or intelligence. People are smart in different ways: Some are smart in being creative; some are smart in dealing with people; some are smart in working with their hands. Everyone has strengths and weaknesses, and not everyone finds academics to be one of their strengths. In fact, many very successful adults did not do well in school.

A child who is struggling with school for *any* reason (an emotional problem, a learning difficulty, poor ability, etc.) needs to find *something else* that makes her feel successful. It could be a sport, a talent, a hobby, or even a strong interest.

In addition, a parent needs to let a child know what special endearing qualities that child has. It could be a sense of humor, gentleness with animals, loyalty to friends, good taste in clothing, a creative imagination, unusual tact, the ability to be assertive, good decision-making skills, being an independent thinker, and so on. In other words, examine a child's personality and point out all the positive things about it *in addition* to mentioning her specific skills or talents.

Of course, if your daughter picks up the feeling that you are terribly disappointed in her lack of achievement, all of the positive comments in the world won't convince her otherwise. If you find yourself not able to let go of strong feelings of disappointment in your child, for any reason, seek consultation with a mental health professional. A therapist can help you figure out what feelings lie behind your particular disappointment.

THE CHILD WHO WON'T ADMIT WHAT HE REALLY KNOWS

Tad began reading at an early age. Now, entering first grade, he's tackling third-grade books. At the end of the first week in school, the teacher calls to tell you that she accidentally discovered that Tad reads, but he's been pretending that he can't read at all!

When you have a chance to talk to Tad about this situation, let him know about the teacher's call. If he doesn't offer an explanation, ask him why he's been pretending he can't read. Of course, what you might get in response is an "I don't know" or a shoulder shrug.

To help him discover a reason, ask, "What do you think would have happened if you'd read in class (or to the teacher) just the way you read at home?" or "Well, what did you think the other kids or the teacher would think if you let them know how well you can read?"

Realize that the most likely reason for a child to cover up his reading (or math) ability when he begins school is the fear of "standing out in a crowd." In this case, the crowd is his classmates. He simply may feel uncomfortable calling extra attention to himself. He might worry that the other children will be put off by his demonstration that he is far ahead of most of them in his reading ability. Perhaps his parents have taught him that it's "not nice to brag," and he equates letting on that he has high ability with bragging.

If your child doesn't come forth with a reason for his pretense (he knew he'd land in the advanced reading group and he doesn't like that group's teacher as much as he likes the teacher who works with the lower reading group), suggest that he might have been afraid to call attention to himself by showing how well he can read. Let him know that many very smart children haven't learned to read when they begin first grade, but some have. Reassure him that showing he already knows how to read well does not mean that the other kids are going to think he's bragging, being weird, or acting like a snob. So long as he doesn't *act* like he thinks he's better than the other kids just because he can read, the class will accept his ability matter-of-factly.

THE ANXIOUS OVERACHIEVER

Melinda is very conscientious about her schoolwork, and she becomes especially tense and worried before a test. Making her usual all-A report card is very important to her, and you worry that she'll fall apart emotionally if she ever makes a B.

Youngsters like Melinda, who seem driven about their schoolwork, are often called overachievers. They become extremely upset with themselves when they don't perform at a superior level. While their perseverence and effort result in high achievement, their success comes at the cost of a high level of anxiety.

Some overachievers concentrate primarily on school success, but many also are just as intense and competitive about out-of-school interests. They tend to be perfectionists, beating up on themselves emotionally when they make a mistake. They expect to be able to do any task in a flawless manner, copying their schoolwork over if there is a smudge or an erasure on a page. Whether it's ballet, karate, softball, or Girl Scout badges, they feel a strong need to excel.

Of course, wanting to excel is a laudable goal. But the problem with overachievers and perfectionists is that they do not excel *comfortably*. Worse yet, they overreact if their performance falls just *slightly* below their goal. It is as if their feelings of self-worth are directly dependent on high achievement, and they tend to become upset or even depressed when they think that they're not measuring up to their own high standards. Actually, it's good for children to experience small failures once in a while in order to learn to cope with the inevitable stumbling blocks and challenges they are bound to face as adults.

If your child tends to overachieve or to be a perfectionist, encourage her to ease up on her expectations. Tell her directly that you would rather she be a happy child and make B's or C's than an A student who is tense and anxious. Reassure her that your love for her is not dependent on her making A's or receiving awards. Let her know that schoolwork is very important, but so is friendship, family closeness, laughter, and time just to be spontaneous. Teach her relaxation skills that she can use on her own to de-stress herself (see "Test Anxiety" discussed next in this chapter).

You might also ask yourself if you serve as a model for your daughter's behavior. If you realize that you tend to be intense, a workaholic, and a perfectionist, it's a good time to reassess your priorities. Start setting an example for your child by taking breaks, joking about little mistakes you make, doing activities just for the fun of it, and relaxing.

TEST ANXIETY

Beth is a bright girl who studies conscientiously. Although she prepares well for tests and goes into the classroom knowing the material, she becomes so anxious that her mind goes blank when the test is being handed out.

Many children (and adults) clutch on tests if their anxiety level reaches a critical threshold. This can happen to greater or lesser degrees: They might suffer temporary memory loss for just a few test items, or they might go blank for the entire test. Frustratingly, they'll remember the answers immediately after the test is over.

A similar phenomenon occurs in some youngsters when they take timed tests. They might perform very well if they are not pressured to work quickly, but will fall apart if someone is timing them.

Unfortunately, such problems tend to perpetuate themselves. Once a youngster experiences test anxiety, he naturally begins to anticipate it for the *next* test. The result is even more anxiety, continuing the cycle. To make matters even worse, the more important a particular test is to a child (for example, a last chance to improve her grade), the worse she's likely to do on it.

Relaxation/Visualization Skills

The best way to help your child overcome test anxiety is to teach her to use a combination of visualization and relaxation techniques. The "anchoring" process already described (see Chapter 2) would be very helpful. Or you could teach her simple progressive muscle relaxation in which you ask her to get comfortable, close her eyes, and then tighten—and then relax—various muscle groups. She can begin by relaxing her feet, and then progressively move the relaxation up her body until it includes her head.

Another way to help a child relax is to use imagery. For example, she could imagine that she's lying on a beach and that soothing ocean waves are washing over her body, each wave increasing the depth of her relaxation. Or you might simply help your child to relax by telling her to make her body like a limp, cooked piece of spaghetti, testing her degree of relaxation by picking up each arm and leg until there is no resistance.

Once a child is relaxed, ask her to imagine a large television screen in front of her. *While keeping herself relaxed,* have her see herself on the screen walking into her classroom, sitting down at her desk, being handed the test, and then working on it calmly and confidently. Once she is able to see the entire sequence without feeling anxious, she can then imagine herself actually *in* the television picture (rather than just watching herself on the screen), feeling what it is like to have this experience of taking a test in a calm manner, answering the questions with a clear, relaxed mind, and then confidently turning in the test paper.

Before you begin to teach her any visualization process, make sure your child understands that a person who first practices seeing herself doing something, in as much detail as possible, is much more easily able to do it in "real life." Top athletes use such techniques all the time to program themselves for optimum performance. Also, let her know that "seeing herself" doesn't mean she will necessarily have actual pictures on the backs of her eyelids; all that is necessary is that she "imagine" or "think about" these images as clearly and distinctly as she can.

Once your child has learned one of these techniques, ask her to practice it at least once each day for several days. This will strengthen the effect. Once she has mastered the process, she can use it the evening before, or the morning of, a test. Most children enjoy these techniques, and feel an increasing sense of self-control as they use them.

Also, be sure to mention your child's test anxiety to her teacher. Most teachers are sympathetic to this problem and will work with your child to help her be as comfortable as possible.

If your child's test anxiety doesn't improve, consult a mental health professional who works with this problem. School is likely to become increasingly miserable for her if she continues to have such a frustrating experience.

IS A "GIFTED" PROGRAM RIGHT
FOR YOUR CHILD?

You receive a note from the school counselor informing you that Betsy's grades and achievement tests qualify her for a special "gifted and talented" program. While you're delighted that she is doing so well, you have some concern about whether or not this special program will put too much pressure on your daughter.

You'll first want to ask the school counselor for more information on what the special "gifted and talented" program entails. In many schools, the "gifted" students are taken out of their regular classrooms for a specified time period each week, meeting together for various enrichment activities. You'll want to know whether or not the special activities are completed in that time period, or if your child will be given extra assignments or out-of-school projects. Also, will she be expected to make up the class work (or homework assignment) she misses during the time she's out of her regular classroom? The point is, you want to get some idea of how much extra work your child will have to do as a result of being in the gifted program.

The next thing to consider is your child's personality. Is she eager to take on challenges and handle the pressure, or is she anxious about her level of achievement? Ask her what she thinks of the program, and whether or not she's interested in it. She might be thrilled and eager, or she might feel pleased that she qualifies but afraid of the extra work that is involved.

If your daughter is uneasy about going into such a program, you have to decide if perhaps she just needs a nudge of support from you in order to bolster her confidence, or if she's likely to continue to feel very insecure about the new arrangement. If you suspect the latter, let her stay in her regular classroom.

But what if your child is highly motivated to join this special program, yet you have your doubts about how she'll handle the pressure? Ask the counselor whether your daughter can try out the new program for a few weeks before making a definite commitment. By presenting the situation to your child as a trial, she won't be as likely to feel a sense of failure if she chooses to drop out.

UPSET OVER NOT QUALIFYING AS "GIFTED"

Lisa is an excellent student and is counting on getting selected for the "gifted" program at school. Unfortunately, her achievement scores slightly miss the mark, and she learns that she doesn't qualify.

Both parents and students are likely to become upset when a child makes superior grades, but can't participate in a gifted program because of an achievement score. This is especially true if the achievement score is still quite high, or if there were extenuating circumstances the day the test was taken (the child's mother went to the hospital that morning, the child was ill, to name a few examples). Of course, schools point out that they have to have a cut-off somewhere, and that wherever that point is, there will be students who will "come very close."

Make sure your child understands that not qualifying for the gifted program doesn't mean that she's not smart. Many very bright kids don't make spectacular grades and/or score below their actual ability level on standardized achievement tests. Also, remind her that she might qualify in the future, as most schools reconsider a child's eligibility for such programs after each year's achievement scores are available.

If you think your child needs the extra intellectual stimulation that would be provided by the gifted program, check with the counselor to find out the after-school, weekend, and/or summer enrichment activities for children that are offered in your community. Or you might plan regular visits with your child to the public library so that she can read up on subjects that pique her curiosity.

Be sure also to acknowledge your daughter's disappointment in not being selected for the special program. Sometimes parents are so eager to get a child over hurt feelings that they try to make light of the situation, making her feel very misunderstood.

When a person has a strong expectation that doesn't get met, disappointment is only normal. Also, you might want to share with your daughter some disappointment of your own when you were in school, letting her realize that everyone has disappointments in life.

Be aware that your child's distress might be heightened if several of her good friends are selected for the gifted program. She might worry that they will reject her, or she might be jealous of their success. Again, acknowledge how difficult this situation is, but encourage her to be just as friendly with the group as she always has been. Remind her that a true friend *wants* her friends to succeed, and can feel happy for them without denying her own disappointment.

AFRAID TO ACHIEVE TOO WELL

Randall is a very bright boy who announces that he will never make A's because he doesn't want his peers to think he's a nerd.

Many youngsters worry that they will be rejected by their peers if they make good grades. They are afraid they'll be viewed as a goody-goody, a teacher's pet, or worse.

In truth, many children who consistently make A's are very well liked. The ones who are rejected are the good students who lack social skills. They might have a superior air because of their high achievement, coming across to their classmates as "know-it-alls." Or they might be children who are very introverted or shy, not putting effort into making friends.

Help your child understand that the key to being well liked by peers has to do more with a youngster's social skills than with how well he does academically. If you can, point out some of his classmates who are both well liked and good students. If you don't know of any such children, cite examples of a child's heroes (athletes or television stars) who would serve as good role models of people who do (or did) well in school and are also very popular.

WHAT ABOUT SEXISM?

Tasha is having trouble with math and is obviously upset about it. When you ask your spouse to help her, you are shocked to hear your mate tell her, "Honey, don't worry about it. Girls just aren't very good at math!"

While it might surprise you, many adults still have sexist perspectives about academic subjects. The common, but inaccurate, notion is that girls won't excel in math and boys won't excel in writing. Or that girls should not be encouraged to participate in sports like soccer or baseball, and that boys should not be encouraged to take dance or gymnastics classes. Such attitudes strongly support traditional stereotypes about what is "feminine" and what is "masculine."

While Tasha's parent expresses this sexist orientation quite blatantly, many parents (and even some teachers) will unknowingly show a more subtle form of sexism. If they don't *expect* a youngster to do well in a particular subject, they are likely to convey this expectation to the student. For example, a teacher may not encourage a girl to work harder in math, but would encourage a boy. Or a teacher may be easier on a boy for his poor spelling or illegible handwriting when she grades his papers, but lower a girl's grade for the same performance. A teacher's or parent's self-fulfilling prophesy about the inherent abilities of males and females can result in a child's not pursuing an interest or skill that she might be quite talented in *if* she had a teacher's or parent's encouragement.

Ideally, both sexes should feel comfortable pursuing any area of interest, both in academics and in sports or recreational pursuits. So examine your own actions to see if you (or your mate) are unintentionally reinforcing this destructive sexual stereotype. If you think your child's school supports this kind of bias, talk with the school's administration about it.

CHAPTER 7

Homework Hassles

MANY PARENTS NOSTALGICALLY THINK OF THOSE LATE-AFTER-noon hours after school as a carefree time for youngsters to relax and play. Whether a child comes home after school, goes to day care, or has other child-care arrangements, the fantasy is that he'll have a snack and then unwind, free to work off the tensions of the day. Evenings, of course, are to be filled with family togetherness, conversation, and fun.

Other parents have a different fantasy about school nights. They see themselves sweetly helping an appreciative, motivated youngster with his homework, imparting their pearls of wisdom to an eager listener.

Unfortunately, such blissful pictures are soon shattered by the reality of the institution called homework. Both children and parents can find themselves hassled, upset, worried, defeated, or downright angry because of it.

Problems can occur because of disagreements between the generations over many issues. *When* a child should do homework and *where* he should do it can become the first conflicts. How much parental assistance is required, as well as the best way to give it, often becomes a source of disagreement not only between a parent and child, but between the two parents. The child who doesn't remember his homework (or the book he needs to complete it), who lies about not having any homework, who says he's completed assignments when he hasn't, who takes forever to do an assignment that he should be able to complete easily in ten minutes, or who finishes his work but never quite gets it back to the teacher can drive a parent wild with feelings of frustration, anger, and/or helplessness.

PARENTS' CONCERNS ABOUT HOMEWORK

Parents can give some subtly mixed messages about homework. While they might publicly state that they think homework is a good idea, some are secretly relieved when a child doesn't have any to do. After all, homework can be a real hassle. It takes some monitoring, possibly even a bit of parental input, and becomes even more time consuming when a child balks or complains about doing it.

With today's busy lifestyles, many parents are relieved that they have one less thing to worry about. The end result is that when a child consistently tells a parent that he doesn't have homework, the parent doesn't double check it with the teacher. As a consequence, the child can end up with the message that homework isn't so important, after all.

On the other hand, many parents get upset when teachers don't give homework on a routine basis. They want a child to become accustomed to the routine of some nightly work, not only to increase his learning, but also to help him develop appropriate study skills. Since he's sure to get homework in junior high and high school, they want him to have some practice in making homework a regular part of his life.

Another concern to many parents arises when a child does his homework in class. Certainly, practicing the material in class is helpful, as a teacher can spot the child who does not understand the assignment. But legitimate homework is *different* from classwork. Parents wonder if the teacher is allowing students to do their homework in class as a means of avoiding developing a richer lesson plan.

Parents also have concerns about the *quality* of homework. Nightly assignments should be designed to help a child master the skills and information he learns in the classroom. If homework is just "busy work," a child can easily become bored, losing whatever original motivation he might have had. A teacher should not assign fifty math problems of the same kind if solving five of them would demonstrate mastery of the concept. Instead, she should design her assignments to have quality rather than length.

ESTABLISHING A HOMEWORK PHILOSOPHY

As soon as possible, you'll want to establish the expectation in your child that he will have homework, and that he will do it. Most teachers begin assigning homework in the first grade, although it usually takes only five or ten minutes to complete. Assignments typically get longer as the child moves up through the elementary grades.

Let your youngster know that adults have jobs and go to work. School is a kid's "work" or "job," and it includes homework.

Also, tell your child that homework will teach him many important skills. He'll learn to plan and to manage his time. He'll also develop a sense of responsibility by learning to remember assignments, complete them, and turn them in on time.

THE STUDY ENVIRONMENT

It's a good idea to get your youngster used to a specific study environment when he starts first grade. Provide a place for him to do his schoolwork, perhaps a desk or table with a comfortable chair. Although older kids often prefer to study in their own rooms, many elementary-school students feel isolated if they are required to do homework away from the rest of the family.

Many parents solve this problem by setting up a place for a child to study in the family room, breakfast area, kitchen, or dining room. Ideally, it would be a spot that is well lighted and free from distraction. Of course, how much distraction is "too much" will depend on the child. Some youngsters require absolute quiet with no visual distraction at all. This type of youngster would not do well sitting where he could see a television, in a room that is also being occupied by a family pet, or working by a window that overlooks an area where other children are playing.

On the other hand, many children can concentrate easily even where background noises or other activities are occurring. Sometimes, parents get caught up in an argument with a child about whether or not the youngster can listen to the radio, or perhaps a cassette or disc player with headphones, while he's doing his homework. To many adults' surprise, some kids actually study more effectively with music or even television in the background. For others, any kind of background noise is disruptive. So if your child brings up this question, let him try working with the auditory background he prefers. If his performance deteriorates, then you can insist that he study in silence.

Also, there are some children who work better *without* a desk or table. They may like the freedom of movement provided by sitting or lying on a sofa or large chair, or even on the floor. If they need a writing surface, they can use a clipboard or some other suitable object.

The point is that it's helpful to have a specific place for studying. It provides a repeated cue for the child that says "this is the place where I do homework," as well as alerting family members not to disturb him when he's in his study spot.

WHO'S REALLY RESPONSIBLE FOR HOMEWORK?

If you could be a fly on the wall at homework time in many households, you might wonder who is really doing the bulk of the work. You would see parents sitting at their children's sides for most of the evening—reading, explaining, dictating, answering questions, and instructing their offspring to do something over again.

You might also notice that whether the adults are patient, irritated, or fuming, and the children are cooperating, complaining, or crying, one thing would be obvious: The kids have 100 percent of the adults' attention. None of the adults would be spending time with their mates, with their *other* children, or simply doing something for themselves. What power those children are wielding!

Of course, the reason parents can get caught up in this trap is that they usually want their children to do well in school. By helping children with homework, parents think youngsters might do better on their assignments.

But when a child turns in homework that is excellent because of a *parent's* contribution, the teacher has no way of knowing what a child does or does not understand about the assignment. She will assume that the child has mastered the material and is ready to move on.

Also, the child whose parent is continually involved in helping him do his homework can become very dependent on this process. Rather than struggle a little and problem-solve, the child gets used to eliciting the parent's help at the first sign of confusion. The end result is that the youngster doesn't learn to think independently, or to have the self-confidence that is built by figuring out for oneself something that is difficult.

This doesn't mean that parents shouldn't help their children with homework at all, but they need to give the minimum help that is necessary. If a child is confused about an assignment, a parent can help him interpret the *instructions* and then watch to see that he is able to do the first problem, sentence, or piece of work. Once this step is done, a parent needs to back off and let the child do the work. Being *available* for help if needed is different from sitting with a child and working on the entire assignment together.

Of course, there are some instances when a teacher will ask a parent to give a child more help with homework. For example, she might suggest that you and your child work with flash cards (such as for sight reading, or multiplication tables) in order to increase your youngster's proficiency in a certain skill. If your child has a learning problem, the teacher might ask you to monitor all homework more closely. If such a request is made of you, be sure to ask the teacher what *specifically* she wants you to do. (For more information on homework help for the child with a learning problem, see Chapter 9.)

Drawing the Line

A good rule of thumb is to check your child's work for *completion* rather than for accuracy. Of course, if his entire assignment is totally wrong, or if he obviously has done the work hastily and sloppily, you'll make sure that he correctly understands what he's being asked to do, and then ask him to do the assignment correctly.

If your child *asks* you to look over an assignment to see if it's correct, go ahead and do so. Point out the items that are wrong, if there are any, and let your child correct them if he so chooses. But give *him* the option of whether or not to correct the errors. This policy makes it clear that homework is your child's responsibility and is less likely to create power struggles over homework than if you *demand* that he redo the incorrect work. Remember, the teacher wants to know how well your *child* is learning. There's no need for you to do elementary school all over again!

If your child's work is illegible, tell him that you can't read what he's written, and that you doubt that the teacher will be able to, either. In this case, you might ask him to redo it. However, many parents demand that a child redo a written assignment because the work is a little messy. Again, it's better to let the teacher be the one to tell him that he needs to work on neatness.

If you actually do need to help your child with homework, make sure the situation stays positive, and stop when it doesn't. You might make a wonderful tutor for *someone else's* child, but your emotional involvement will probably result in your losing your objectivity with your own. A good rule of thumb is that if *either* you or your child frequently ends up yelling and/or in tears, let someone else help him with homework. This person might be the other parent, an older sibling or other relative, or a teenager in the neighborhood.

If you create a negative teaching situation for your child, he's not likely to learn effectively, and he will probably feel bad about himself ("What's wrong with me?" or "I must be stupid,") and think he's a disappointment to you. He might also begin to rebel against doing schoolwork not only at home, but in the classroom as well.

AN EFFECTIVE MOTIVATION STRATEGY

There are many tasks in life that might not be intrinsically motivating, yet we have to do them. Yearly preparation of income taxes could easily fall in this category. Chances are that homework, at least some of the time, will fall into this category for your child. So how can you best motivate him to do something that he needs to do, but might not want to do?

Many people try to motivate themselves to do something they really don't want to do by imagining themselves doing the task and telling themselves things like "I should," "I have to," "I must," or "I ought to." Unfortunately, this tactic isn't very motivating, and it can actually cause a person to rebel against his own good intentions.

What works better is to anticipate the *positive consequences* of getting the task done. You might tell yourself something like "Won't it feel great to have that finished!" and then create a mental picture of yourself as you would feel *after* you've done it.

Applying this strategy to homework, you can teach your son to tell himself something like "Won't it feel great to get this done so I can play!" —and then make a mental picture of himself putting his homework into a folder and going out to play. It's very important that he include both steps of this process: *telling himself* something positive about the outcome, and *making a mental picture* of himself having that outcome while *feeling wonderful* about it.

By teaching your son this simple positive motivation strategy, you'll increase the likelihood that he will do his homework, even when he doesn't feel like it. Of course, you'll also want to let him know that he can use this same process to get himself to do *any* task that he's reluctant to do like cleaning his room or practicing a musical instrument.

COMMON PROBLEM SITUATIONS

LYING ABOUT HOMEWORK

Whenever you ask Jeff if he has homework, he either denies that any was assigned or tells you that he finished it in class. Now you've just received a progress note from the teacher telling you that Jeff is failing because of his numerous missing assignments.

Most parents in this situation are upset to discover that their youngster hasn't been doing his homework, but they are even more appalled by the fact that he has been consistently lying to them. Adults reason that a child ought to realize that he can't keep hiding the fact that he's not doing his homework, as the truth is bound to come out. So why would a smart child lie about this, knowing that he'll eventually be caught?

The truth is that children have magical thinking which allows them to believe that they just *might* get away with not doing homework without their parents ever finding out. They will hang on to this fantasy until they are caught, continuing to think, "I'll get away with this one more time." Such self-delusion is common in elementary-school children, and it does not mean that a child is going to have character problems as an adult.

Of course, some children lie about homework because they feel inadequate to do it. Rather than admitting that they're having a hard time in school, they develop the "Who cares?" stance as a defense. Again, evaluation may be necessary to see if the child is having genuine academic difficulty.

A child's lying about homework can also be an expression of anger or rebellion, although these motives are likely to be out of his conscious awareness. As with any time you suspect that your youngster is rebelling, you'll want to look closely at your family life to see if something is going on that could be creating such feelings. Of course, the source of the anger might not be able to be prevented (perhaps you're involved in a divorce, an older sibling is getting lots of recognition, or there's a new baby at home). The point is, pinpointing the problem allows you to help your child bring his feelings out into the open for discussion, and gives you a chance to give him information, support, and reassurance.

Whatever the reason behind your child's behavior, you'll want to make the point that his lying has made things worse. Set a negative consequence for the lying (such as loss of television privileges or earlier bedtime) for a brief period of time in addition to the consequences you set for his not doing his homework.

Making Sure It Gets Done

One of the most effective ways to make sure a child is doing homework and turning it in is to design an appropriate behavior contract (contracts are described in Chapter 5). In this case, the target behavior would be the child's "completing and turning in homework." Again, the teacher would give you this information on a daily basis, perhaps by making a check mark and signing her name on a child's assignment notebook or other paper. You would then give your youngster a daily positive or negative consequence as a result of the teacher's report.

For example, if the teacher has checked that all homework due that day was turned in, the child might earn time on a computer or video-game player, or might earn so many minutes of television viewing. If the teacher reports that homework was not done, the child would be required to do the missing assignments that evening in addition to his regular homework, and would not get any special privileges.

Remember that the child's "privilege" might be one that he already has, but *now* must earn (watching television, having his radio playing as he falls asleep). However, some youngsters will require that you *add* a privilege or incentive that will motivate them. This can occur because there is nothing in their regular routine that will motivate them to change if you take it away, or because they are the type of child who will rebel more if they can't earn an extra, nonroutine privilege. This matter very much depends on the individual child.

However, once a youngster is consistently turning in his work, it's likely that his grades will improve, he'll get along better with his parents, and his self-esteem will rise. When this happens over a period of time, the idea is that he will become self-motivated through his success and not require a behavior contract.

The behavior contract approach prevents a child from lying to you, and it also keeps those missing assignments from piling up until he's failing. Teachers usually like this system because it takes only a brief time at the end of the school day to make a check or check-minus and sign their initials.

The Forgetful Child

For the child who has been doing his homework but forgetting to take it to school, or misplacing it, it's helpful to give him a special folder for his homework. Many kids require this extra boost to help organize themselves. Otherwise, they might stuff papers into their jeans back pocket, into a mass of other papers in a large notebook, or into an already messy desk. The usual result is that they are unable to locate their work when the teacher asks for it. It's also wise to require your child to pack up his schoolbooks and materials the night before each school day.

When your child demonstrates that he's doing and turning in his homework consistently, you can switch to a weekly teacher report, and then "graduate" him from the monitoring system if he continues to perform well. If the same problem begins again, you can reinstate the behavior contract. Some children will need to continue such a system for some time, even for several grades. Without this structure, they will simply slip back into disorganization until they mature a little. While parents obviously hope they won't have to use such a system for very long, the alternative of having a child who fails and/or is in constant trouble in school is even less appealing.

SLOPPY WORK

Gil frequently turns in homework that is sloppy or illegible. Testing has ruled out the possibility that he has fine-motor coordination problems; his handwriting is poor due to carelessness. You're worried that Gil's teacher thinks you're an uncaring parent or, even worse, that you aren't even paying enough attention to notice that he's turning in sloppy work!

You'll need to come up with a reasonable standard about when homework is neat and legible enough to be acceptable. Talk with the teacher and let her know that you do care that your child's work is sloppy, but that you haven't considered it bad enough to force the issue. Ask her advice about whether or not she wants you to change your policy. If she wants you to enforce a stricter standard, be sure to let your son know that the new arrangement is at the *teacher's* request (if he's not involved in the discussion).

Remember that you can use an incentive system for your child's having neat, legible homework, allowing him to have some privilege for meeting the standard without your having to ask him to redo it.

THE "LAST-MINUTE" BOOK REPORT

Sally keeps up with her daily work, but she has been warned about her habit of leaving book reports to the very last minute. Just as she's going to bed, she suddenly gets a panicked look, remembers that she has a book report due the next day, and tells you that she still has to read the last chapter of the book!

If the problem is fixable by a child's staying up an hour or so later than her usual bedtime, and if she's not too tired, you might decide to let her finish the book and write a quick report. But often in such situations, hours would be required for the child to finish a book report and have something acceptable to turn in to the teacher the next day.

In the latter case, many parents flip into high gear to get the work finished. While complaining or lecturing to the child about how she needs to plan ahead (for the umpteenth time), the parent essentially does the major part of the work.

However, the way a child might actually learn to plan ahead is to experience the natural consequence of her lack of planning. Parents who jump in to finish a youngster's work for a deadline rob her of this critical lesson. What will occur, in most cases, is that a teacher will mark a late book report a few points lower, maybe even a grade lower, because of lateness. A stricter teacher might even give her an F. It's highly unlikely that a child will fail a grade in elementary school because of a late book report, but there are certainly penalties that must be paid.

Of course, if your child is normally conscientious and occasionally makes the human mistake of forgetting, it's reasonable for you to put forth a major effort to help her out of a bind. You might stay up with her and *help,* still not doing the work for her. But if your youngster tends to be irresponsible about deadlines despite being given several reminders, you will be helping her more if you resist the urge to make everything perfect for her by completing her assignments. Instead, investigate her system (or lack of system!) for writing down her assignments, and teach her how to effectively use an assignment notebook or calendar.

PUTTING OFF DOING HOMEWORK

From the time he gets home from school, Ron keeps assuring you that he is going to do his homework "in just a little while." Before you know it, his bedtime is fast approaching, he still isn't studying, and you end up yelling at him to start doing his work. You're tired of feeling like the world's biggest nag and of ending so many evenings being angry at your son.

Sit down and talk with Ron about the homework issue. Tell him you know that he's probably as tired as you are of all the hassling that goes on about it, and you want to find a way that he can do his studying without your having to nag or yell at him. Then ask him for his suggestions.

If he comes up with an idea that appeals to you, tell him he's got a great idea and then put it into action. For example, sometimes children will suggest that they do their homework as soon as they finish a snack after school. By getting this responsibility over with, they don't have to worry about it all evening.

However, many kids want to relax and unwind after a long school day. For them, it would be torture to have to plunge right in and do homework right after they get home from school. This type of child might suggest as "study time" the hour before dinner, giving himself some time to play and relax before settling down to work.

If your child doesn't come up with an appropriate suggestion, you might ask him to agree to a deadline by which he must *start* his homework. For instance, if he has not begun his homework by seven o'clock, everything else stops for him at seven o'clock (television, phone calls, playing) and he begins his homework. When he finishes (but not until), he can resume his usual activities.

With this system, a child has a good bit of flexibility. But he must also plan ahead. If it's important to him to see a seven o'clock television show on a particular evening, he'll have to forfeit some afternoon playtime so that he can finish his work before the show begins. Otherwise, he just might have to see his program twenty minutes after it's begun, or perhaps even miss the entire show. Be sure that your child understands that he must *finish* all of his assignments before the designated study period ends.

By using one of these approaches, your son gets to have some choice about when he will study. At the same time, you are assured that he won't leave his homework until the last minute, and that you won't have to ruin your evening worrying about it. The key is to stick to the agreement you and your child have reached.

DAWDLING OVER HOMEWORK

Misty is a master at taking fifteen minutes of homework and dragging it out into a two-hour ordeal. She uses every excuse to interrupt herself, needing a drink of water, having to go to the bathroom, getting a tissue, sharpening her pencil, asking unrelated questions, etc. You know that she dreads doing her homework just as much as you dread watching her go through this torturous process, but how can you get her to stop avoiding the inevitable?

First, you might want to rethink your child's study environment. She might need to study in a room by herself, free of all distraction. This can also motivate her to finish her work quickly so that she can rejoin the family. If she's already studying in such a place, however, why might she be avoiding getting her work done?

Typically, children avoid homework because they feel overwhelmed by the amount or uncertain about their ability to do it. There are also youngsters who gain a great deal of adult attention, even though it's often negative, by fooling around instead of settling down to work.

Let your daughter know that you are sympathetic to her feelings by saying something like "Honey, I know you hate to spend so much time doing homework. I'm going to show you a way to get it finished faster." Using a kitchen timer or stopwatch, get her to set appropriate time goals for *sections* of her homework, and then see if she can beat her own deadlines. The deadlines can be moved up as she is ready, gradually decreasing the overall amount of time she'll have to spend doing homework.

It's very important that *your child* set her own goals, and that they be achievable. As an example, suppose that she has ten math problems to do. Ask her how long she thinks it would take her to finish those problems *if* she really concentrated and did not let anything distract her. If she suggests a time limit that you don't think she can *easily* make, encourage her to make it longer. The point is, you want her to *succeed* in meeting her own goal so that she gains a feeling of confidence and achievement.

At first, let her set a specific time for each *subject* in which she has homework. If she has math, spelling, and social studies, she will set the timer three separate times. Later, when she's used to handling the smaller chunks of work successfully, you can encourage her to set the timer just once and complete all her work in that time period.

For many children, just the idea of beating the timer is reinforcing. Even so, many parents like to offer a youngster a small incentive for getting work completed before the timer dings. One example that most kids like is to offer a nickel or dime for each unit of work that is completed on time, letting the child save up the earnings to buy something special. If you object to using money as a reward, allow your child to earn time watching her favorite video, having a parent read to her, getting a backrub, or staying up a certain number of minutes past her usual bedtime.

Using a timer for the homework dawdler seems to help by serving as a mechanism for the child to focus her attention. In fact, teachers have learned a similar method for helping a child work more efficiently in the classroom. They will place a stopwatch, or even a regular watch with a second hand, on a child's desk while she's doing classwork, and simply ask her to time herself on how long it takes her to complete the work. Just keeping track of the time in this way often helps a child work more efficiently, and can even help motivate her to shorten her work time, if appropriate.

Teaching a child to break up her homework into small units by using a timer also can help her feel less overwhelmed about the amount of work she has to do. Also, the idea of "beating her own time" seems like a game, perhaps making homework a little more fun.

TOO DEPENDENT ON YOUR HELP WITH HOMEWORK

Patrick continues to want you right by his side when he's doing homework. If you try to leave him to do something else, he quits working and calls you back to help him. Now that he's in fourth grade, you're getting concerned that he can't seem to work by himself.

When a child is too dependent on a parent for help with homework, the parent probably has unintentionally taught the youngster this habit. Typically, the problem begins when a child enters first grade. The parent finds it fun to sit with the youngster for the five or ten minutes it takes to complete the nightly assignment. Having the parent right there with him, the child naturally begins to ask for help when he's stuck.

By the time a child is older, say in fourth grade, his homework takes much longer. It's not so much fun anymore for a parent to have to sit through an entire homework session, and the parent is likely to have a growing sense of uneasiness about the child's inability to work independently. But the habit is well entrenched.

This problem can also occur after any time period when a child genuinely needs some extra help from a parent. He may be working well by himself until he runs into a stumbling block, such as multiplication tables. A parent might work with him for a few weeks specifically on multiplication, only to find that the child becomes accustomed to the parent's help and wants it to continue indefinitely.

If you realize that your youngster has become too dependent on your help with homework, you'll need to begin weaning him from this type of consistant attention. Be up front with him about the fact that you have other things you want to do in the evenings, and that he really needs to learn to do his own homework. Start him off in the evening with one piece of his assignment, explaining that you're going to do something else and that you want him to come and find you *after he's finished* that portion of his work. When he brings you the completed piece, designate another section of work for him to do in the same way.

As your child gets used to working independently in short spurts, gradually lengthen the amount of work you want him to do before he checks in with you. Eventually, he'll be doing all of his work, coming to you only after he's completed an entire evening's assignments.

Be sure that he understands exactly what he's supposed to do with each piece of work *before* you leave him to work on his own. If you need to help him with a concept, do so; let him do one or two examples, and then leave him alone to finish that section. If he keeps asking for help or comes to get you before he's finished the section, tell him you will not look at the work until he's given *his* answers for the entire section. If his work is totally wrong when he brings it to you, explain the concept again and then ask him to redo that section of work.

If you want to, you can always add an incentive to this process. By successfully working on his own, he can earn a special privilege that's agreeable to both of you.

DOING HOMEWORK WITH A FRIEND

Jill and another fifth-grade girl down the street are good friends and have been doing their homework together after school almost every afternoon for a week. Now you're wondering if this is such a good idea, since studying together seems to be becoming an expectation on the part of the two girls.

If the two girls are good, conscientious students, if they are completing their assignments, and if their grades are being maintained at their usual level, then there's probably no harm in allowing them to study together. On the other hand, if you see that the girls are goofing around and not getting their assignments done properly, if their grades are dropping, or if one of them is really doing most of the work and the other is copying, it would be best to have them get together *after* they've each done their homework independently.

If the friend is a mediocre or poor student, you might allow your child to help her out *occasionally*. However, you don't want your youngster to be in the uncomfortable position of having the friend depend on her to become a personal tutor. Of course, if *your* youngster is a poor student, you don't want her to become dependent on having her friend spoon-feed her assignments, and you'll want to insist that she study independently most of the time so she'll learn to figure things out for herself. A nice compromise might be for the girls to do their assignments separately and then get together to check their work.

DOING A PROJECT WITH A DISLIKED CLASSMATE

Alexandra is infuriated because her teacher assigned her to work with a girl she can't stand. She wants you to ask the teacher to assign her another partner.

Unless the disliked child has a history of bullying your child, let Alexandra know that you will not support the idea of asking for a change. Explain that there are people in every school, job, or situation whom one might not like. However, one still has to learn to work with those people, and to be able to cooperate with all types of personalities. While you can be sympathetic to her preference for having someone she really likes as a project partner, you can remain firm in your decision that she needs to work through this challenge.

Point out to your child that she may not really know this girl very well, and that working with her on the project might give her a different view as the two of them get to know each other better. Even though there are things she dislikes about her classmate, she may well find other things about the girl that she can respect.

Also, your child might have formed her impression of the other youngster from a rumor or a stereotype (a different race, religion, economic level), and should be encouraged to judge each person as an individual rather than listening to rumors or thinking in stereotypes.

PUTTING OFF LONG-TERM PROJECTS

At the beginning of the grading period, Pam was told that she would have to complete a science project that would be due at the end of it. Now it's a week before the project is due, and she hasn't even started it. Of course, she's panicking and begging you for help.

Let this be a learning experience for Pam. Ask her to tell her teacher that she put off the project until the last minute, and now she must ask for a new deadline. You can best help by assisting her to focus on what her project will be about, figuring out how she'll go about getting the necessary information and materials, calculating how long it should take her to complete the project, and so on. Of course, she'll probably get a somewhat lower grade for her tardiness, but that is part of the learning experience.

Pam's dilemma also calls for some *preventive* measures. Even adults often have difficulty organizing themselves for a long-term project, and adults, unlike young children, have a good conception of time. So plan ahead to teach your child the skills that are involved in doing a long-term project the next time one is assigned.

For example, hang a large calendar in your daughter's room. This will help her to make a concrete representation of time. When a project is assigned, put a mark on the date it is due. Then, looking at the number of weeks between the day it is assigned and the date it is due, help your youngster design an appropriate plan. Resist the urge to lay it all out for her; instead, get her actively involved in planning each step. What does she think she should do first? Then what?

As your child comes up with ideas, mutually decide on a due date for each step toward the project's completion. For example, she might have a topic selected, along with ideas about where she can get the information or materials she will need by the end of the first week. At the end of the second week, all of her materials will be gathered, and so on. By structuring your child in this step-by-step manner, you'll be teaching her a good strategy for organization that she'll be able to use the rest of her life.

CHAPTER 8

When Your Child Doesn't Want to Go to School

YOU PROBABLY EXPECT THAT YOUR CHILD WILL GO TO SCHOOL without much fuss, even if she is not especially thrilled with the idea on any particular day. After all, once she's enrolled, she knows that school is a nonnegotiable fact of life.

Just imagine your frustration if your child should continue to balk about such a routine event. Even worse, imagine your sense of helplessness if she simply refused to go to school at all!

Unfortunately, these scenarios happen all the time. Whether your youngster tells you directly that she doesn't want to go to school, makes up various excuses about why she *can't* go to school, or simply refuses to go, you'll want to correct the problem as quickly as possible.

Most parents in such situations immediately assume that something has gone wrong at school. They suspect that there's a problem with a teacher, with other school personnel, with another student, with the curriculum, or with the school environment. While this may be the case, in many instances a child's unwillingness to go to school may be related to family issues rather than to school itself. Even if a child points to something at school as the cause, realize that her perception may hide the *real* dynamic, which often is not in her conscious awareness.

For example, a child suddenly might not want to go to school, complaining that she's afraid of some of the boys in her class. But the real reason she's upset might be that there's a new baby at home, and she's jealous of all the attention the baby will get while she's away at school. Or perhaps she senses some marital tension at home, and is fearful that her mother and father are going to divorce. She might believe that if she stays home, she'll be able to prevent her parents from fighting or splitting up.

She might even be picking up on the fact that her mother is having anxieties or problems of her own and would feel safer if the child stayed home with her, even though the mother is probably not conscious of having such feelings. In each case, realize that the child's true underlying feelings are often out of her conscious awareness. Consequently, she really believes the problem is at school.

At the same time, a child who doesn't want to go to school can be genuinely upset by something that *is* going on there. Common situations include a fear of not doing well academically, problems relating to peers, negative feelings about a teacher, having to participate in some disliked activity in physical education, anxiety about having to give an oral book report or to participate in a play, problems on the school bus, sensitivity about being corrected in class, concern about not being able to get to a bathroom in time, worry about disciplinary consequences for misbehavior, and more.

Remember that a child's teacher can be an excellent resource for understanding what might be going on with a child who stops wanting to go to school. Chances are that if the problem is really being created at school, the teacher will be aware of it.

A MIXED MESSAGE?

Before looking at the common reasons why children balk at going to school, you might want to examine the messages you give to your child about the importance of school attendance. Many parents pay lip service to the notion that school attendance is paramount, yet their behavior sends a mixed message.

For example, many parents plan vacations or out-of-town visits during times when school is in session, even though they could have selected a different time. Or they might be lax about getting a youngster to school on time, allowing a child to be tardy much more often than is necessary. Some parents even tell a child that he's not going to school on a particular day because it is inconvenient for that parent to take him.

It's not that occasions don't occur when it might be preferable or necessary to take a youngster out of school, or when a youngster might be tardy for a very legitimate reason. The point is that it's helpful to look at the subtle messages you might be giving your child unintentionally about the importance of school attendance.

COMMON PROBLEM SITUATIONS

NOT FEELING WELL ENOUGH TO GO TO SCHOOL

Rebecca has begun to complain of frequent stomachaches and nausea in the mornings before school. Your pediatrician assures you that there is no physical reason for her complaints, and suggests that the cause is stress-related. Now when she says she's ill in the morning, should you send her to school or let her stay home?

Many children develop symptoms of illness that stem from emotional causes (called psychosomatic illnesses) rather than from physical disease. However, it's important to remember that the child's physical distress is *real* even when the cause has emotional origins. Take the common tension headache as an example. The cause is stress, but the pain is certainly very real.

By understanding that genuine physical symptoms can be caused by emotions, you won't make the common mistake of telling your child, "Your tummyache is all in your head!" Although there is the possibility that a child could be pretending to have such symptoms, most often, the distress is really there. In all likelihood, her tummy really does hurt, and she really does feel nauseous.

Explain to your child that you know she feels ill, and that her body is trying to give her a message. Such symptoms reflect a warning that something is bothering her, although she might not be consciously aware of it. Since she does not have a physical disease which the other children could catch, she needs to go to school in spite of her discomfort. Remind her that you (or her other parent) go to work despite various aches, pains, or symptoms that keep you from feeling your best, so long as you don't have an actual illness.

Give your daughter whatever medication your doctor has suggested to help her be more comfortable, but insist that she go to school. If she's worried about vomiting at school, your trying to convince her that she won't is unlikely to work or to give her much consolation. Instead, give her a plastic Ziploc bag to keep in her pocket or purse to use in the event that she does vomit and can't make it to the rest room in time. Chances are that she'll never use the bag, but having it handy can help her feel more confident.

When It Might Be Real

But what if your child tells you that she knows she's coming down with some illness, that *this time* is different from all those other times her stomach hurt? Or what if you are concerned that this one particular time, she's actually getting sick? A practical way to handle this common problem is to take your child's temperature. If she has a reading of 100 degrees or more (people can psych themselves into a temperature of 99 degrees without any illness being present), let her stay home from school. Otherwise, reassure her that she doesn't have a fever, and send her to school.

"But what if she really is sick and develops a fever at school?" might be your next question. While it's true that your child *might* develop a fever later that day, the school will call you if that occurs, and you can bring your youngster home. If you make an error in the other direction, keeping her home "just in case" when she's not actually ill, you reinforce her using this mechanism to manipulate you in the future.

If these suggestions seem a little harsh to you, remember that we're talking about a child who is in danger of missing a lot of school by using physical complaints, consciously or unconsciously, as an excuse to avoid something that's troubling her.

Instead, you want her to figure out what's bothering her, if possible. Even if she can't figure it out, you want her to learn to deal with the situation and not become an adult who avoids responsibility because of stress or emotional issues.

While you can manage your child's psychosomatic symptoms in this way, you'll want to get to the emotional root of the problem. Ask her to tell you what she thinks her body could be warning her about, whether something is bothering her inside. For example, ask her, "What do you think your stomach is trying to tell you when it hurts that way?" If she has no idea, offer some of your own. Is she worried about a test, a certain subject, her teacher, or some misbehavior? Is there something bothering her about her family, or about herself? Has something happened that she's afraid to tell you about for fear that you'll be angry with her? Let her know that, whatever the problem, nothing could change your feelings of love for her.

If your child continues to have emotionally caused physical distress and you can't pinpoint or solve the problem, consultation with a mental health professional is recommended.

CHRONICALLY "GETS SICK" AT SCHOOL

Lexie has developed a habit of suddenly feeling ill at school and wanting to go home. You've checked out the possibility of a physical cause with your pediatrician, who assures you that Lexie is physically fine. But the school keeps calling you to pick her up.

Talk with the counselor and ask for the school's help with this situation. Many schools solve this common problem by sending a child to the school nurse (or to whomever fulfills this function), who then takes the youngster's temperature. If she has a fever, the parent is called. If she doesn't, she's told to lie down in the nurse's office until she's feeling better, perhaps also having a cold washcloth applied to her head or a hot-water bottle placed on her stomach or back. About every thirty minutes, the nurse encourages the child to go back to class.

This procedure usually works well for several reasons: The child gets some attention and nurturing; she learns that people who don't feel well but aren't really "sick" are still expected to follow their normal routine; she discovers that she can't manipulate her way into going home; and she finds that it's really quite boring to lie in the nurse's office without any company! If consistently followed, this plan typically results in a child's staying in class without complaint.

Of course, you'll want to address the underlying cause of your child's wanting to come home from school. The information discussed in the above section (Not Feeling Well Enough to Go to School) also applies to a youngster who becomes "ill" at school.

AFRAID TO GO TO SCHOOL

Trisha has been waking up the past few school mornings with vague complaints of not feeling well enough to go to school. She begs you to let her stay home, becomes obviously more distressed if you push her to go, and promises convincingly that she will go to school the *next* day. But the next day is the same story, and she finally admits that she can't make herself go to school because she feels scared.

Obviously, the first thing you would do is question your child about the source of her fear. She might come up with a concrete reason. For example, she might tell you that her teacher is unfair to her, that she's being bullied on the playground by an aggressive peer, or that she is supposed to give an oral book report and is petrified at having to get up in front of the class and talk. With such information, you can help her work out a solution to the problem, perhaps with the teacher's or counselor's help.

But many youngsters who are scared to go to school (technically called school phobic) will not have a specific reason to be frightened. Often their complaints are very vague ("I don't know, Mommy. I just get a funny feeling when I go into the school" or "The kids just make me nervous, but I don't know why"). Of course, even when a youngster mentions a specific reason that sounds logical, that reason might turn out to be a smokescreen. This can occur because children often *don't know* why they are scared. Their behavior doesn't make sense to them, either, so they might search for a reason to give their fear some legitimacy.

If your child mentions a specific fear and you take measures to fix the problem, her fear should disappear when the difficulty is resolved. For example, if a bully really is picking on her and the teacher takes steps to reassure her that she'll no longer be picked on, her fear of going to school should end. If she continues to feel scared, perhaps giving you yet *another* complaint ("The room is too hot" or "I get dizzy standing in the lunch line"), chances are that school is not the source of her anxiety.

In the case when your child's fear cannot logically be explained by anything that's happening at school, it's likely that she's suffering from some form of separation anxiety. This means that she is having psychological difficulty *not* with going to school, but rather with having to *leave* home. But why would this be?

Causes of Separation Anxiety

Many children who experience separation anxiety are afraid that some harm will befall a family member, often their mothers. Typically, their fears might include worrying that a parent will become ill or die, perhaps from a car accident. Or they might worry that a tornado will strike their house and kill everyone in the family, leaving them all alone in the world.

These types of fears may stem from unconscious anger toward the person who is the source of worry. For example, let's say a youngster is angry at her father, is unaware that she's angry with him, and she momentarily imagines that something awful would happen to him, perhaps that he would be hurt or killed. Feeling guilty about such a thought, the child begins to worry that she will be punished. What worse punishment than for her father, whom she really loves, to be killed in an accident? Most likely, she will not recognize any of these feelings at a conscious level. She'll be genuinely confused about why she is suddenly so overly concerned about her father's welfare, unaware of her underlying anger toward him.

Closely related is the child who worries that *she* will suffer some harm, rather than being anxious about the fate of a parent. She might worry that she will get lost, kidnapped, ill, and/or killed. In other words, she thinks she deserves being hurt. Consequently, she wants to remain close by a parent in order to feel safe. Again, these feelings are likely to surface because of some guilt the child is carrying.

Another common source of a child's separation anxiety is a parent, typically a mother who does not work out of the home, who gives a subtle message that she needs the child to stay home with her due to the *mother's* fears. The mother's wish that the child not leave her home alone is usually totally unconscious, and the mother might protest in all sincerity that she *does* want her child to go to school. In such a case, the mother has a conflict between a *conscious* part of her that certainly wants her child to go to school and to grow up normally, and an *unconscious* part that wishes the child would stay a baby and stick close by her. Psychotherapy is often needed to help such a mother become aware of her inner conflict and the reasons behind it.

Of course, younger children (preschoolers) whose mothers work outside the home sometimes develop separation anxiety because they pick up on their mothers' guilt about not staying at home with their youngsters. By having problems being left at school, these children unconsciously exert a lot of power in feeding their mother's guilt. Sometimes this same dynamic may still be at work when the child goes to elementary school.

A child's separation problem can also be a reflection of an inner wish, conscious or unconscious, *not* to grow up. She might fear the responsibilities of adulthood, deciding that it would be much easier just to stay a child. Her need to stay home where a parent is available and/or where the child can remain in familiar surroundings represents a way to remain more childlike, and to have a parent take care of her needs.

A child's fear of growing up can have many sources. For example, parents might be experiencing financial or marital difficulties that make a youngster feel that it's scary to be a grown-up. If she's on the verge of adolescence, your daughter might find the whole notion of sexuality to be very frightening, preferring to stay a child rather than to mature into a teenager who must grapple with sexual feelings and issues.

Sometimes a child's separation anxiety serves as a means to control something that is going on at home that she doesn't like. An example would be the youngster who decides that if she stays little and dependent on her parents, they'll simply *have* to give her more attention. Or perhaps she's worried that her parents might not stay together, and thinks, as stated earlier, that staying home will magically keep them together. Again, such thoughts and feelings are often totally out of a child's conscious awareness.

If your child is experiencing separation anxiety, you'll certainly want to discover the source of her concerns. Gently explore the possibilities mentioned above, giving appropriate information and reassurance. At the same time, you want to make sure that your child continues to go to school.

Getting the Child to School

The child who says she's too scared to go to school will typically beg and plead with a parent to be allowed to stay home. She might say something like "Just one more day at home, PLEASE!" or make convincing pledges like "I'll go back Monday, I promise!" If a parent insists that the child go to school, the youngster will often become even more fearful, perhaps crying, shaking, or trying to hide. She might even become hostile and rebellious, threatening that she will hate the parent forever if made to go to school, or even engaging the parent in a physical struggle on the way to the car. She might reluctantly get in the car without a fuss, but resist getting out of the car when she arrives at school. Some children will cry and cling to a parent while walking into the school, or will refuse to let go of a parent once the parent tries to leave the child at the school or at the classroom door.

At this point, you might wonder if it wouldn't be better to let your child stay home from school for a few days, rather than go through the hassle of insisting that she go when she's obviously so upset. You might think that the break will not only increase her motivation to return to school, but that she will appreciate your understanding support and will reward you in turn by going to school without a fuss.

Letting a child with separation anxiety stay home, even for

a few days, is almost always an error. Since her problem really has nothing to do with school, staying away doesn't lessen her scared feelings. In fact, staying home can actually worsen her anxiety because she has been allowed to be more dependent on a parent's presence. The longer a child stays out of school, the more difficult it can be to get her to go back.

The best approach is to remain insistent that she go to school. Remain calm and compassionate, but stay firm. If one parent has been used to taking the child to school in the morning, it often helps to have the *other* parent perform this task. If it is impossible for the other parent to do this, or if there is only one parent available, recruit an older teenage sibling, an adult relative, or even a trusted neighbor to see to it that the child gets to school.

Just this simple change in procedure can make a tremendous difference in a child's level of cooperation. It breaks up the power struggle element in the child's relationship with the parent who usually takes her to school, and sends a very clear message about the importance of attending school.

Every effort should be made to get the child into the car or bus. A young child can be easily carried if she will not walk on her own. However, it is *not* recommended that a parent get into a physical battle with a child who is too big to control easily. Such struggles can end up with someone getting hurt, and it is traumatic for both parent and child to get into a wrestling match. This is why it can be helpful to have someone other than the usual parent (most often a mother) take the child to school—preferably a larger, stronger adult. The youngster is much less likely to begin a physical struggle when the odds of success are stacked against her!

If the child arrives at school and refuses to get out of the car, the driver can explain the situation to an adult who is nearby and request that the person ask the counselor or principal for help. Someone on the school staff will come out to the car to get the child and escort her into the school building. When this happens, the child will usually go willingly.

What happens if you're able to get the child to school, but she remains highly reluctant and shows little improvement? What if you can't get the child to the car in the first place? Immediately arrange an appointment with a mental health professional. When you call to schedule the appointment, be sure to tell the receptionist that you cannot get your child to school. Since this symptom can become so much worse the longer the child is out of school, mental health professionals consider this to be an emergency situation, and will work you in for an immediate appointment.

PLAYING HOOKY

About an hour before you plan to leave to pick up Stan from school, the doorbell rings. You find a very sheepish Stan accompanied by a policeman. It seems that Stan and a friend had played hooky that day!

After thanking the officer for retrieving your son, you'll obviously want to sit down with Stan to discuss this situation. In all probability, you'll be angry, hurt, and/or confused, but resist the impulse to become highly emotional. You'll have plenty of opportunity to tell your child how you feel about this situation after you're calmer and you've heard what he has to say.

It's wise to ask your child to tell you exactly how he decided to leave school, and to account for his activities during the day. After all, your reaction might be quite different after you've heard his story.

A child might have a variety of reasons for this behavior. He could have had a test that day, was unprepared for it, and left school to avoid a likely failure. A popular peer might have planned to play hooky and approached him to go along, and your child felt that he couldn't say no. He might have seen a television show that portrayed two kids having a great adventure by skipping out of school, and he thought it would be fun to have a similar experience. Perhaps he and his friend got in trouble at school for some misbehavior, panicked, and left before they got caught. It could be that your child hates school, and his running off represents a form of discouragement or rebellion.

The point is, many adults tend to assume that a child's skipping school represents an act of defiance by a child who is headed for some kind of big trouble, like juvenile delinquency. While this *could* be the case, it could also be a serious overreaction, especially if this is your child's first time to leave school. Many perfectly normal children have such an experience.

Your reaction to this situation will also depend on how your child and his friend spent the day. Contrast how you'd feel if you found out that the two children spent the day at the zoo versus discovering that they were persuaded by some teenagers to go to a nearby apartment and smoke pot.

Also, be sure to ask your child if anything frightening or abusive occurred during the day. If he was victimized in some way, he might be especially afraid to tell you about it, fearing that he is to blame for having put himself in a situation where this could occur. You can ask about this by *calmly* saying something like "Did anything frightening happen to you, or did anyone hurt you or make you do something that was scary or uncomfortable? It's okay for you to tell me if something happened; I'm not going to be mad at *you* if something like this happened."

Obviously, you'll gear your reaction to your child's specific situation, whether the issue is the fear of making a low grade, a vulnerability to peer pressure, a rebellious attitude, or so on. Unless he remains cocky or defiant, it's probably not necessary to give him a negative consequence for this first-time offense; he's likely to be scared and to have learned his lesson from getting caught. Instead, give him a clear message that leaving school is totally inappropriate and can expose him to danger, and that you *will* give him some serious consequences (such as restriction of privileges for a number of weeks) if he repeats this behavior. Let him know that if he has any problem at school that tempts him to leave, he should immediately call you or talk to his teacher, counselor, or other school personnel.

TAKING A DAY OFF

Barbara awakens one morning and asks you if she can take the day off from school. She says that she has no tests and that she already knows what her homework is and will do it, but that she just wants to stay home for one day and get a little break from school.

You might, like many parents, feel that this shouldn't even be an issue, because you wouldn't think of allowing your child to stay home from school unless she is ill. However, many parents see no harm in an *occasional* "mental health day" away from school. They just wonder under what circumstances it should occur.

The factors to consider involve a child's previous absences, how well she is doing in school, and her attitude toward school. If she basically likes school, has a good attendance record, conscientiously keeps up with her work, and is easily passing all her subjects, you might grant her wish and allow her to stay home one day. Of course, if she's an overly dependent child and you think her request is disguising some other problem, it would be best to insist that she go to school.

If you do decide to allow your child to stay home due to her request, make sure she realizes that this is only a once- or twice-a-year choice. Also, in your note to the school the next day, don't say that your child was *ill*. You don't want to start a pattern of covering up for her by lying. You could truthfully say something like "Julie just wasn't up to going to school yesterday, and I gave her permission to stay home" or, more directly, "Julie really needed a 'mental health day' yesterday, so I chose to let her stay home."

If the school considers the truth to be an unexcused absence, your youngster should be prepared to accept whatever consequences will occur. So be sure you and your child understand the policy for absences before making a decision about the "day off."

CHAPTER 9

When Your Child
Needs Special Help

THERE ARE MANY REASONS WHY A CHILD MIGHT NOT BE GETTING what he needs in school. The youngster might be having problems academically because of one or more common factors: his particular learning style; a learning/language difference (the more current term for learning/language disability); an attention deficit disorder (called ADD); an attention deficit disorder with hyperactivity (called ADDH); inappropriate behavior; or emotional problems. Since poor performance in the classroom can reflect any combination of these factors, psychological and educational evaluation are usually required to determine the cause of a youngster's specific difficulties. Even if a problem appears to stem from obvious behavioral or emotional causes, testing will sometimes reveal the presence of an underlying learning problem.

Depending on the nature of the problem, a youngster might be eligible for a variety of special programs in the school. Some school counselors also offer time-limited groups for children who share similar difficulties. For example, groups might be held for children whose parents are divorced, who are in stepfamilies, who have had a family member die, or who have problems in social skills. Some schools also offer tutoring sessions before or after school, or during the lunch hour, for youngsters who could benefit from them. And many schools also have speech therapists available for children who need these services.

Parents also have the option to get academic help for a child through private resources in the community, such as tutors, learning specialists, speech/language pathologists, educational psychologists, and occupational therapists. Parents can consult mental health professionals (psychiatrists, clinical psychologists, social workers, licensed counselors) for youngsters who have behavior or emotional problems. As mentioned, many children will require help in both areas. Parents also have the option to explore legal measures if they think the school is not adequately addressing a child's needs.

Please note that *each* of the topics in this chapter can, and does, fill thick books. The information given here is not meant to represent a thorough discussion of each issue, but rather a brief practical *overview*.

LEARNING STYLES

We all have a preferred way to learn, although we might not be consciously aware of it. Our brains take in information through the five sensory channels, but one is usually predominant in processing the information we receive. A person's choice in most situations is either visual, auditory, or kinesthetic (movement and touch); taste and smell usually only play a minor role in the majority of learning situations.

In a typical classroom, the majority of children will have enough visual, auditory, and kinesthetic *capacities* to learn their work effectively. However, a few students will have one preferred mode and very little capacity in the other two. If the content of the material taught is not presented in their primary mode, they will find it difficult or impossible to process the information. When a teacher presents a concept in all three modalities, some children will be confused, necessitating that the teacher repeat the concept using the child's most efficient modality. When a teacher does not do this, the one-modality child often will have gaps in his understanding due to his missing bits of relevant information.

The Visual Child

The child who learns visually is often organized, neat and orderly, and observant. He can be quiet, is more deliberate, and is less distracted by noise. He is typically a good speller and will prefer to read than to be read to. He remembers what he *sees,* and often has trouble remembering verbal instruction. He learns most effectively when he is given an overall view and purpose as well as a vision for details.

The Auditory Child

The primarily auditory child is usually easily distracted and often talks to himself. He is likely to move his lips or to say his words when reading. Spoken language is easy for him, but math and writing are usually more difficult. This child learns by listening, and memorizes by steps, procedure, and sequence. He often speaks in a rhythmic pattern, likes music, and can mimic tone, pitch, and timbre. He learns by talking to himself both out loud and internally, and tends to remember what was *discussed.*

The Kinesthetic Child

The child who is primarily kinesthetic is physically oriented and moves a lot. He often touches people and stands close to them. He learns by doing and memorizes while moving and seeing. He often points when reading, gestures a lot, and learns through manipulating and doing. His handwriting might be thick and pressured. He may be very intuitive, but not care much about detail. He will remember the over-all impression of what he *experienced,* rather than remembering what was seen or what was discussed.

Teaching to Children's Learning Styles

A good teacher will present classroom material in ways that involve all three primary modalities. For example, when teaching the alphabet, she might put a letter on the board for the children to identify, ask them to call out or touch items in the room that begin with the sound of the letter, have the class draw a picture of the letter, trace it, touch a raised letter (for example, a letter made out of sandpaper), or cut out its shape.

Although teachers generally are accustomed to presenting material in the visual and auditory channels, many tend to overlook the kinesthetic channel, especially in the older elementary grades. This is especially likely to occur if a teacher places a high priority on a child's working quietly at a desk for much of the school day.

However, many teachers are beginning to see the wisdom of allowing children to work on a section of carpet, lying or sitting on pillows if they so wish. "Hands-on" learning, or learning by *doing,* is becoming more popular than the traditional and more passive method of having children spend large amounts of their classroom time using workbooks at their desks. Children also are being grouped around tables while they work together on projects, moving about as needed. Although teachers of the early elementary grades are more likely to allow their students more kinesthetic freedom, fourth- and fifth-grade teachers are beginning to see the merits of such approaches. Since it is estimated that the majority of dropouts in the school system are youngsters who are strongly kinesthetic, such changes may well make a dramatic difference in the kinesthetic child's satisfaction with school.

The point is that if your child is having an academic problem, you might question if he is one of the estimated 12 to 20 percent of students who only learn in one sensory channel. You'll want to be sure he is being taught in a manner that utilizes that channel, and you can often help him compensate for a deficiency in a particular subject by presenting the material in a manner that emphasizes that channel.

How a Parent Can Help

If your child is visually oriented, he'll probably learn to spell better with flash cards than with phonics. Or if he cannot remember the content of a story read out loud to him, ask him to visualize (make a mental movie of the story in his head) while you are reading to him.

If a highly auditory child has trouble comprehending a story while reading it himself, suggest that he mentally *talk* the key words of the story in his head as he's reading. Also, teach him to stop reading after short intervals and *rephrase* the material in his own words. Let him listen to instructional learning tapes on a subject that's difficult for him to understand.

If your child is primarily kinesthetic, encourage him to move and gesture as he explains what he's trying to learn. Let him "act out" a story, playing the different characters and changing positions as he does. Let him stand up, sway, or pace as he learns the material (but remind him that if he's allowed to do this in the classroom, he must find a way to do so without disturbing other students). Remind him to stop once in a while as he studies and do something physical, perhaps highlighting his material or writing a brief outline or summary of it. If he has difficulty with his handwriting, teach him to type at the earliest opportunity.

If you determine that your child learns best in a particular way that is not being taught, be sure to share this information with his teacher. Sometimes just paying attention to a child's primary learning channel and utilizing it will clear up his difficulty with a particular subject.

LEARNING/LANGUAGE DIFFERENCES

A child with a learning/language difference is a youngster of *at least* average intelligence who does not master specific language/learning skills that are expected for his age. Often, he will show real discrepancies in his performance, scoring easily and well in some areas, but much lower in others.

Children with learning/language differences can, though not necessarily, also have problems with hyperactivity and/or attention problems (see discussion in next section). Many also have immature reflex patterns (diagnosed by a pediatric neurologist) and can be hypersensitive to touch. They may be very impulsive, a factor that contributes to behavior problems. They might also persist in repeating certain topics or activities over and over, as if their brain circuits have jammed (called perseveration). These children are also at higher risk to develop behavior and/or emotional difficulties, although these problems can often be alleviated or lessened with early diagnosis and appropriate intervention.

Unfortunately, many parents take a wait-and-see approach

with a young child in hopes that he'll "grow out of it." They plan to address the problem, if it hasn't disappeared, by the time a child is in third or fourth grade. While it's never too late to begin working with a child, and much can still be done in later grades, it's far preferable to get a problem diagnosed as early as possible (when a child is four of five). Then he won't be as likely to suffer self-esteem problems and/or turn off to learning due to the frustration, discouragement, and feelings of failure that typically accompany youngsters who can't stay up with their classmates but are not given special help or support. He also will be less likely to miss out on the basic language/reading skills that provide a critical foundation for learning.

However, some children's learning problems simply don't surface until they are approximately in fourth grade. The reason is that, up until that time, youngsters are usually given classroom tasks requiring a student to perform only *one* operation. In fourth grade, suddenly they are expected to *integrate* several learning processes. For example, rather than looking up an answer and recording it verbatim from a textbook, a fourth-grader might be expected to read several paragraphs and then make an *inference* in order to arrive at the correct answer. Consequently, if your child who's always done reasonably well in school suddenly begins to have trouble in about fourth grade, you still need to consider the possibility that he might have a learning/language difference.

What Are They?

There is no system of classification of learning/language differences on which all educators agree. However, one system that is widely used and relatively easy to understand is based on what the brain must do in order for learning to take place. The first step is *input:* Information gets into the brain through the five senses. The second step is *integration:* The brain needs to make sense of the information that has arrived. The third step is *memory:* Information must be stored and retrieved. The fourth step is *output:* The brain must send some kind of message back to the nerves and muscles.

Using these four steps, we can describe learning/language differences for each as follows:

Input

When a child has problems with information coming in through one or more senses, he is said to have a perceptual problem. The problem can be with visual perception (what he sees), with auditory perception (what he hears), and/or with tactile perception (what he feels). Examples of a visual input problem would be specific reading disorders in which the child is unable to perceive and recognize letters or groups of letters; reversing letters (b for d, q for p); or transposing letters (*was* seen as *saw; dog* seen as *god*); difficulty in focusing on what is significant instead of on other aspects of the visual background (pictures on a page distract him from what is written); or problems judging distance (knocking over a drink because his hand reaches too far).

Examples of auditory input problems would include a child's having difficulty distinguishing subtle differences in sounds (he hears *bill* instead of *bell*); difficulty focusing on specific sounds when there are other sounds in the background (he doesn't hear what is said to him because the television is on); problems processing sounds as fast as most people (he misses part of what you are saying because he can't keep up); or following lengthy commands (the teacher gives *several* assignments for homework, only some of which he completes).

Integration

At least three factors are required in order to understand information coming into the brain: sequencing, abstraction, and central auditory processing. Sequencing involves registering information in the correct order, and can be visual, auditory, or kinesthetic. Examples include understanding whether it's *d-g-o, g-o-d,* or *d-o-g* after the brain has correctly "seen" the letters; being able to tell a story with the events in the right order; knowing what day comes after Wednesday without going back over the entire list of days beginning with Monday; or not running from first base straight to third base in a baseball game.

Abstraction involves being able to infer meaning from the context in which a word is used. For example, a child might read or hear a story about a dog. If the teacher then asks the child to tell her something about the dogs in his neighborhood, he is unable to answer her question because he can talk only about the dog in the story, not dogs in general.

Central auditory processing has to do with a child's ability to *understand* what people say to him. His hearing ability is fine, sometimes even extrasensitive, but the sounds he hears become scrambled in the brain. These youngsters have difficulty listening to or maintaining attention for speech delivered in a complex environment or not spoken clearly. Consequently, they perform best when instruction is presented in the simplest terms possible, and when a teacher has their undivided attention.

Memory

Once information has been received and integrated in the brain, it must be stored in order to be retrieved later. There are two types of memory: short-term (remembering a phone number that Information gives to you), and long-term (remembering a phone number whenever you need to use it). Of course, memory problems can occur in the visual, auditory, or kinesthetic modes.

Output

Information comes out of the brain either by means of words (a language factor), or through muscle activity (writing, drawing, gesturing). A youngster with a language problem might have difficulty initiating conversation (spontaneous language), or responding to someone else's conversation (demand language).

A child with motor problems might have trouble with large-muscle movements (perhaps being clumsy, bumping into things, or having problems with physical activities like running, swimming, or climbing), known as gross-motor problems. Or he might have trouble with tasks that require many small muscles to work together in an integrated way (as in writing), which is called a fine-motor problem.

How do you know if your child has a learning/ language difference?

As you can see, learning/language differences can be an extremely complicated subject, and most children who have them will have problems in several areas. Only a thorough professional evaluation can determine whether a child has a *diagnosable* learning/language difference and, if so, what specific types of problems exist.

If you notice aspects of your child's behavior at home and in school that might suggest the need for such an evaluation, mention them to your child's teacher. A diagnosis can't be made based on an isolated characteristic, however (for example, it is common for children to reverse some letters up through first grade; this does not mean a child has "dyslexia" or some other learning difference). Also, many children may have slight problems in these areas, but not enough to require special-education intervention. A qualified professional doing an evaluation will know, based on norms for children of the same age, when a problem necessitates special intervention.

Attention Deficit Disorder

The term Attention Deficit Disorder (ADD) is relatively new, but the syndrome it describes is not. It used to be called *hyperactivity,* but recent research has found that some children with ADD show no symptoms of hyperactivity at all. Those who do show hyperactive behavior are commonly classified as Attention Deficit Disorder with Hyperactivity (ADDH).

Youngsters who have learning/language differences may or may not have ADD, but almost all ADD children have learning/ language differences. Basically, ADD children have problems with focusing and attending; ADDH youngsters *also* have difficulty with impulse control. According to the American Psychiatric Association's diagnostic manual, a child must have *at least eight* of the following symptoms in order to be classified as ADD or ADDH:

- Often fidgets with hands or feet, or squirms in seat.
- Has difficulty remaining seated when required to do so.

- Is easily distracted.
- Often blurts out answers to questions before they have been completed.
- Has difficulty following through on instructions.
- Has difficulty sustaining attention in tasks or play activities.
- Often shifts from one uncompleted activity to another.
- Has difficulty playing quietly.
- Often talks excessively.
- Often interrupts or intrudes on others.
- Often does not seem to listen.
- Often loses things.
- Often engages in physically dangerous activities without considering possible consequences.

Of course, many children exhibit one or more of these symptoms. It is the number and the severity of such symptoms that are taken into account in deciding if a specific child should be diagnosed as having ADD or ADDH. Many youngsters outgrow these disorders by adolescence, others do not.

Unfortunately, some parents whose children are ADD or ADDH dismiss this possibility by pointing to the fact that the child can sit quietly and watch a television program in its entirety. They reason that if a child has attention problems, he wouldn't be able to do this. Although this thinking is understandable, it simply isn't accurate. Television seems to have a special stimulating quality that can attract the attention even of the child who normally has attention problems, and it should not be used as a diagnostic indicator.

It is very important that parents of ADD and ADDH children understand that the child's attention, concentration, and impulse control problems *are not something the child is doing willfully*. Consequently, punishment is not appropriate. However, this does not mean that such a child should not be accountable for specific misbehavior (being aggressive toward other children, lying, or being defiant). Some of these children will try to use their diagnosis as an excuse for inappropriate actions that are perfectly well within their control, and they need to receive consequences for their inappropriate behavior just like any other child.

Treatment

Current treatment of the ADD or ADDH child usually involves teaching his parents a behaviorally oriented child-management approach combined with medication prescribed by a pediatrician, child psychiatrist, or pediatric neurologist. While parents naturally have concerns about putting a child on regularly administered medication, the drugs used are very helpful in making it possible for a youngster to focus his attention and to take the edge off his impulsiveness.

Many reluctant parents have consented to a child's being given a *trial* on medication, and have been so impressed with the positive changes that they wouldn't think of discontinuing the medication until the child is ready (determined by periodic trials off medication, usually during the summer vacation from school). Parents often worry that such medication will tranquilize a child into a sleepy, lethargic state, but when the medication is properly administered and *titrated to the dosage a specific child needs,* the youngster remains alert and energetic. Obviously, parents should make the decision about putting their child on medication only after exploring their questions and concerns with their child's physician.

In addition to the traditional methods of treatment, biofeedback has recently become another recognized treatment for ADD and ADDH. Diet changes (most commonly, restricting a child's intake of sugar and red food dye) also have been reported to be helpful with *some* children.

WHEN YOUR CHILD NEEDS
AN EVALUATION

Many school districts provide intellectual, educational, and/or psychological evaluation for its students. Typically, authorization for testing must come through the counselor or the principal. You might initiate the request to have your child evaluated, or the school personnel might suggest it to you. Schools must have parental consent before they can test a child; a parent always has the right to have a youngster evaluated at a community agency or by a professional in private practice, rather than by the school's diagnosticians. The parent might also opt to use such private resources for a second opinion after the school has performed its evaluation.

The Evaluation

Throughout evaluation, your child's performance will be interpreted in light of her cultural background, primary language, level of cooperation and motivation, and any handicapping conditions she might have. Her scores might be affected by a temporary state such as fatigue, anxiety, or stress. Disturbances in her neurological, personality, and/or temperamental makeup will also affect her scores. For these reasons, it is important that you see your child's performance as representing an *estimate* of her current functioning in *the areas tested.*

Your child probably will be given an intelligence test to assess both her competencies and her limitations. Rather than being a *group administered* IQ test, such as those that are sometimes administered in the classroom, a thorough intellectual assessment will be done. The most widely used individually administered intelligence tests for elementary-school children (the WISC-R or the WISC-III) examine a child's abilities in a *variety* of tasks, both verbal (vocabulary, general information, capacity for abstract thinking, etc.) and nonverbal (putting puzzles together, finding what's missing in a picture, assembling blocks to make a design, etc.). These tests also estimate the level of a child's distractibility. The IQ score itself makes only a general statement about a child's current level of intellectual functioning (diagnosed as metally retarded, below average, average, bright, superior, or very superior); it is the *pattern* of a child's performance on the various tasks that allows meaningful inferences about her capabilities and weaknesses.

Your child probably also will be tested in several educational areas. She'll receive tests that assess her performance in various skills necessary for reading, spelling, and math. Tests of language development and usage and of perceptual organization may also be included.

Psychological aspects of an evaluation might include structured and/or unstructured personality tests. Structured tests would be those where your child is asked direct questions about her feelings and preferences. Unstructured tests might consist of her making up stories to pictures, drawing, or looking at inkblots and telling the examiner what they look like to her.

Preparing Your Child for Testing

If a full evaluation is required, your child might spend several hours with a psychologist or educational specialist. Since young children often have short attention spans, the child might be seen over a number of sessions rather than performing all tests in one appointment. The length of time you can expect between the testing and the time you'll be called for feedback is highly variable, sometimes taking weeks, so it's best to ask when you can expect to hear something about your child's assessment.

It's wise to tell your child that he is going to be tested in advance so that you can answer his questions about it and help put him at ease. But you might wonder what exactly you should tell him about *why* he is being tested.

It's best to be perfectly honest about the reason. Some examples might be: "You've been having some trouble with your reading, honey, and the testing will help us find out how your teacher can help you so that reading will be easier for you"; "The teacher has noticed that it's really hard for you to stay in your seat (keep from talking out loud in class, concentrate on your schoolwork, and so on). This testing can help us understand why you are having this trouble so we can help you correct it"; "Johnny, I know you're tired of getting into trouble at school for arguing and fighting with other kids. This testing is to try to figure out why you are having trouble controlling your anger"; or simply, "This testing will show us how to make school easier for you."

Let your son know that the testing will help you *and him* to understand better both his strengths and his weaknesses. Help him to be curious about what his abilities are, and let him know that you will give him information about the test results as soon as you know them.

Feedback

Ideally, the person who performed the tests, the school counselor, or the teacher will give your child feedback about the testing. Although the discussion will naturally be more detailed for an older child, even first- and second-graders need to be given some brief feedback about their strengths and weaknesses. Find out if this happens, and discuss with your son how he feels about the results. If one of the school personnel will not talk with your child about his tests, you certainly can. When a youngster is included in knowing the results of his evaluation, it helps him to have a more positive attitude about such evaluations and makes him feel important and included.

In most states, parents are allowed by law to receive copies of these types of evaluations. It is useful for you to have a copy for future reference, in case your child should need educational or psychological help as he gets older.

It is also recommended that you *ask* the person doing the assessment for a feedback session if one is not offered. Even if you've received a copy of a written report, you'll probably get much more information if you have a chance to ask questions and to get clarification from the person who writes the report.

Parents' Fears About Testing

Sometimes parents are hesitant to have a child tested because they are afraid the child will somehow be upset by the process. However, children usually enjoy the testing, or at least are neutral about it. Many things they are asked to do are similar to school activities (vocabulary, math, and so on); other tasks are presented more like games. Also, the person administering the tests has been trained to perform the evaluation in a way that supports the child's feeling good about his performance. The fact is that many parents unnecessarily make testing into a big deal, while kids easily accept it. In fact, when a child has unnecessary anxiety about it, it's likely that it is the *parent* who has the problem!

The child who does become upset *during* testing is usually upset about the school-like tasks. He might worry that he is doing poorly, or he may balk at being asked to perform tasks he doesn't even like doing in school. Obviously, this type of child is already having the same upsetting feelings about his schoolwork, so it is very valuable to find out the kind and extent of the difficulty he is having. However, even when a youngster becomes upset with or has trouble on a particular task during testing, he will be helped by the examiner to leave the session feeling good about his efforts.

WHAT DO YOU TELL A CHILD WHO HAS A LEARNING/LANGUAGE DIFFERENCE?

The most important point you want to get across to your child is that having a learning/language difference *does not mean that he's not smart*. By definition, a learning/language difference means that he's at *at least* average or above average in intellectual capability. In fact, even some youngsters who fall in or above the *superior* range of intelligence can have specific learning/language differences.

Let your child know that having a learning/language difference means that his abilities are uneven. For example, he might read at a level that is two years above his grade, but may fall almost a year below his grade in math. Also, he might show uneven performance in the same subject from one day to the next, understanding a concept and then losing it until he's been exposed to many repetitions.

While you'll be sympathetic to his frustration, remind him that everyone has strengths and weaknesses. Be sure that he understands his strengths, both academically and personally, and remind him that many highly successful adults have or had learning/language differences.

WHAT CAN BE DONE TO HELP?

Many schools have special programs available for children with learning/language differences, and there are also public and private resources. Early treatment intervention is ideal, since a young child's self-esteem can be greatly affected by an experience of not doing well in first grade. Consequently, many communities are beginning to develop special programs for preschool "at risk" youngsters.

However, even if a learning/language difference isn't diagnosed until late in a child's school career, intervention can still be helpful. It is never too late to begin working with a youngster who has learning problems.

Teachers and educational specialists who have specific training to help youngsters with learning/language differences will, of course, work on the areas of difficulty. Perhaps more important, they will identify a child's *strengths* and help him to use those strengths to compensate for his weaknesses. These professionals have many alternative strategies available to help a youngster with problems in reading, memory, spelling, math, writing, language development, and/or organization skills. Also, occupational therapists use many techniques that are very helpful for children who have fine-motor, gross-motor, or sensory-integration problems. Whereas some children will, with appropriate intervention, be able to eliminate their learning/language difference in time, many will only be able to learn special techniques to compensate for their weaknesses.

A CONTROVERSIAL NOTE

You should also know that some educators think that children with learning/language differences, or at least some of them, might not have problems in school if their teachers were trained to use the learning *style* most suited to each child (discussed above). These critics of the current educational system think that, rather than our children having *learning* disorders, perhaps our schools have *teaching* disorders.

Moreover, a school of thought is developing that many youngsters who have been diagnosed as having learning/language differences only have these problems because of one or a series of emotionally loaded experiences as a young child that led them to *decide* that they had such problems. For example, a child might experience a teacher or parent telling him that he is stupid, yelling at him when he didn't understand something, and his young mind concludes that the adult is correct. In other words, he makes a limiting decision, which soon drops out of his conscious awareness, and continues to repeat the same type of problem. This example makes the point that the negative things adults unthinkingly say to young children can have a lasting impact, necessitating great caution on our parts about the messages we give our youngsters.

Evidence of the strength of such negative impressions comes from recent informal reports of successful interventions (using neurolinguistic programming) with adults who had great difficulty in school, were diagnosed as having various learning problems, and were often placed in special-education classes. When the origin of their negative beliefs and limiting decisions about their abilities in school was remembered and released, they became able to do well or excel in tasks that they could never before perform successfully. For example, a "dyslexic" student who could never before see letters correctly reportedly now reads easily, with no difficulty seeing the letters in words. It is hoped that more evidence will appear in the near future to confirm the usefulness of this new approach, and to specify the conditions under which it applies.

THE SPECIAL-EDUCATION OPTION

Once your child's evaluation is completed, a recommendation might be made for him to receive some type of special services that come under the umbrella of "special education." Generally, schools have a meeting, called an ARD (Admission, Revision, and Dismissal), with parents, teacher(s), the counselor, principal, and other school staff to determine the appropriate individual educational plan (called an IEP) for the child.

It is very important that you (both parents, ideally) be at your child's ARD meeting, if at all possible. However, many parents become intimidated when they attend these meetings, simply because they had no idea so many people would be present. Remember, you *are* a most important part of this meeting. Be sure you ask questions, clarify issues, and—most important—voice your opinions about what is being planned. You'll then be asked to sign a consent form for whatever plan is to be implemented.

ARD's are held at least once a year, whether the issue is admitting, continuing, or dismissing a child from a special-education program. Goals are set for the current year after a child's progress has been discussed. An ARD meeting also can be called at any time during the school year, either by the school or by a parent who feels that the current plan needs changing.

What Are the Choices?

Options for special education vary greatly from one school district to another. The most common goal, however, is to keep a child in the regular classroom with his peers as much as possible. In a recent policy called "inclusion," special-education teachers come into the classroom to work with the special-education children. More traditionally, the child might be allowed to leave the classroom temporarily to go to a resource room set aside for help whenever he runs into difficulty, or he might spend one class period or more in the resource room on a daily or semiweekly basis. The most extreme placement is a self-contained classroom, where a child is placed full-time with other children who have similar difficulties. This class is usually taught by a teacher who has special training in working with children who have learning/language differences, attention deficit disorder, behavioral or emotional problems, or specific handicapping conditions.

The quality of special-education programs varies widely from school to school. Consequently, you'll want to be very clear about exactly when, how, and by whom your child will be assisted. It is helpful to visit the particular class situation that is being recommended for your child in order to get a firsthand impression of what your child will experience. Remember, you do have final say-so about whether your child participates in a special-education program.

You might wonder whether a private school would have more to offer a child who has learning/language differences, since private schools usually have fewer children per class than do public schools. Although there are certainly exceptions, many private schools do not have the resources or staff for the special-education programs these children need. In fact, many times youngsters who have just been diagnosed with a learning/language difference will *leave* a private school in order to take advantage of the greater special-education resources usually available in public schools. A smaller class really isn't the only answer for such a child.

If you are considering a private school for your child with a learning/language difference, be sure to be up front with school personnel about your child's difficulties. In addition to asking whether or not the school has special programs for children with learning problems, also ask about what type of *modifications* they can and will make to meet your child's specific needs. It's also wise to observe the class in which your child would be placed, as well as any special programs in which he would participate, and compare them with the public school's program.

How Will My Child Feel About Special Education?

Many children who are recommended to self-contained special-education classes worry about rejection and ridicule from their peers. Some youngsters are concerned even about leaving their regular class to go to "resource" for a short period of time during the school day.

The truth is that other children often *do* make fun of children who are in special-education programs, especially older students. Telling your child that he shouldn't be concerned about this happening just sets him up to distrust you. It's better to prepare your child for the fact that some children might tease him, but that he should respond in the same manner as he would respond to any other type of teasing (see Chapter 4). For example, he might say something like "You don't know what you're talking about!" or "I just need a little extra help right now."

Point out to your child that the relief he's likely to feel about his school progress once he is able to receive appropriate help will offset any teasing he experiences. Once he becomes involved in his new program, gets accustomed to the new teacher, and makes new friends, he usually will come to accept the arrangement. When this doesn't happen, it is usually the *parent* who has not made the adjustment.

PROFESSIONALS WHO CAN HELP

Whether help is recommended after evaluation, or if you decide to seek it on your own, there are many professionals who work with children who are having difficulty with some aspect of school. Physicians include pediatricians, pediatric neurologists, and child psychiatrists. Mental health professionals include educational and clinical psychologists, social workers, and licensed counselors. Speech and language therapists and occupational therapists also do helpful work with children who have learning problems.

If you need the services of any of the above professionals, do not pick someone out of the phone book. Get a referral from someone who knows that professional and the quality of his or her work. Good sources for referrals are your pediatrician, family doctor, minister, rabbi, the school, a nearby university department that specializes in the field you need, or, of course, a person who has received the services of that professional, and whose judgment you trust. Many communities also offer referral lines from various professional associations, although you will usually only be given several names from a list of licensed professionals. A more personal referral tends to provide you with more information about a professional's personality and quality of work.

THE LEGAL OPTION

What about the rare occasion when all your efforts to resolve an issue with a school still leave you dissatisfied?

What Is the Law?

In 1975, a landmark in education was passed with Public Law 94–142. This law says that states must provide free, *appro-*

priate education for all children, and serves as a financial, administrative, and enforcement policy. It also allows for federal aid to reimburse state and local education agencies for a portion of the additional costs of providing special education.

This law provides services for children if they have difficulties in hearing, speech, vision, learning differences, chronic or long-term health issues, emotional disturbance, mental retardation, and physical impairments. It also contains sections pertaining to the specific appropriate educational processes for such children, as well as precise requirements for their identification, evaluation, and placement.

Resolving a Dispute

There are several avenues available if you do not agree with a school's educational plan for your child. First, you can get an independent evaluation by a professional who does not have any connection with the school. If those results support your position, you can ask for another meeting with the school personnel to discuss your child's individual educational plan. If the school does not modify its position, your next step could be to make a written appeal to the school district's bureau of special-education appeals. This group might suggest mediation between your point of view and the school's.

If mediation is unavailable, of if it doesn't succeed in a satisfactory compromise from your viewpoint, you can ask for a more formal administrative hearing. The next step, should you need to take it, would be filing a complaint to the state education department, a complaint to the federal Office for Civil Rights, and/ or a lawsuit.

If you decide to take any of these measures, be sure to be prepared to back up your claims with facts. It is wise to keep a file on your child's educational, medical, and family history, including copies of previous evaluations and a record of all your communications with the school. You might also talk with other parents to see if they share your concerns. The possibility of class action can be quite persuasive to even the most reluctant school system.

Understanding your legal rights to have input into your child's education means that you can truly be your child's advocate. Locate the advocacy offices and law information centers in your area that can give you information and assistance about your legal rights. These resources can also recommend attorneys who concentrate on special-education law, if needed (for those names, see _Help Me to Help My Child_ by Jill Bloom in the Suggested Reading list that follows).

Suggested Reading

American Psychiatric Association. *Diagnostic and Statistical Manual III-R*. Washington, D.C.: American Psychiatric Association Press, 1987.

Bloom, Jill. *Help Me to Help My Child*. Boston: Little, Brown, 1990.

Cleveland, Bernard. *Master Teaching Techniques*. Portland, Oregon: Metamorphous Press, 1987.

Gregory, Cynde. *Child Made*. Portland, Oregon: Metamorphous Press, 1990.

Grinder, Michael. *Righting the Educational Conveyor Belt*. Portland, Oregon: Metamorphous Press, 1989.

Ingersol, Barbara. *Your Hyperactive Child*. Garden City, New York: Doubleday, 1988.

Jensen, Eric. *Superteaching*. Portland, Oregon: Metamorphous Press, 1988.

Kline, Peter. *Everyday Genius: Restoring Children's Natural Joy of Learning—and Yours Too*. Portland, Oregon: Metamorphous Press, 1988.

Levinson, Harold M. *Smart but Feeling Dumb*. New York: Warner Books, 1984.

Loyd, Linda. *Classroom Magic*. Portland, Oregon: Metamorphous Press, 1988.

O'Connor, Joseph. *Not Pulling Strings*. Portland, Oregon: Metamorphous Press, 1987.

Ostrander, Sheila, and Lynn Schrode. *Superlearning*. Portland, Oregon: Metamorphous Press, 1987.

Silver, Larry. *Attention Deficit Disorders: A Booklet for Parents*. Summit: CIBA Pharmaceutical, 1987.

———. *The Misunderstood Child*. New York: McGraw-Hill, 1984.

Tureki, Stanley, and Leslie Tonner. *The Difficult Child.* New York: Bantam, 1989.

Van Nagel, C. et al. *Megateaching and Learning Techniques.* Portland, Oregon: Metamorphous Press, 1985.

Walker, Eugene, and Michael Roberts. *Handbook of Clinical Child Psychology.* New York: John Wiley, 1992.

Index